Reform of the International Institutions

The IMF, World Bank and the WTO

Peter Coffey

Emeritus Professor, University of St Thomas, Minnesota, USA

and

Robert J. Riley

Professor of Economics, University of St Thomas, Minnesota, USA

Edward Elgar
Cheltenham, UK • Northampton, MA, USA

Published by
Edward Elgar Publishing Limited
Glensanda House
Montpellier Parade
Cheltenham
Glos GL50 1UA
UK

Edward Elgar Publishing, Inc.
136 West Street
Suite 202
Northampton
Massachusetts 01060
USA

A catalogue record for this book
is available from the British Library

Library of Congress Cataloguing in Publication Data

Coffey, Peter.
    Reform of the international institutions: the IMF, World Bank and the WTO/
    by Peter Coffey and Robert J. Riley.
        p.   cm.
    Includes bibliographical references and index.
    1. International finance. 2. International Monetary Fund. 3. World Bank.
    4. World Trade Organization. I. Riley, Robert J., 1963–   . II. Title.
    HG3881.C5827   2006
    332.1'5—dc22

                                                                2006002684

ISBN-13: 978 1 84376 026 9
ISBN-10: 1 84376 026 6

Printed and bound in Great Britain by MPG Books Ltd, Bodmin, Cornwall

Contents

Preface: The Reasons for Writing this Book

Rarely has a more opportune moment arrived for the writing of a book. It is, in 2004, exactly 60 years since the original negotiations were held which led to the creation of the IMF and the International Bank for Reconstruction and Development (now more commonly known as the World Bank) – but not the WTO. Since that date (and particularly since the so-called 'concordat' of the 1980s), so much has happened, and even the most benign observers would be forced to admit that the IMF and the World Bank have lost sight of their original mission. Thus, even before the publication of Joseph Stiglitz's highly critical book, *Globalisation and its Discontents*, in 2002, the authors of the present book had decided to embark on a study of the three international organisations. However, unlike Professor Stiglitz, though agreeing with many of his critical observations, the present authors try to offer different solutions for the many problems currently facing the international community. Also, unlike Professor Stiglitz, the present authors look at the problems and offer solutions from both American and European points of view – whilst, at the same time, taking into account the views of countries in other parts of the world. According to colleagues in different countries, it is this approach – apart from the timing of publication – which sets this book apart from similar publications. Also, as has already been observed, the original Bretton Woods trilogy was incomplete in that whilst the IMF and the Bank for Reconstruction and Development were created, no trade organisation was set up. Instead, the General Agreement on Tariffs and Trade was signed – backed up by a small secretariat in Geneva, Switzerland. Surprisingly, maybe, this treaty worked rather well and was mainly responsible for the successful organisation and conclusion of a number of major trade rounds. More recently, nevertheless, a real trade organisation has been created, the World Trade Organisation (WTO), which, in its relatively brief existence has (to put it mildly) raised the hackles of many groups – notably in Seattle.

Consequently, in this book, all three organisations are examined and proposals made for their reform. Thus, in Part I, they are analysed from an independent European viewpoint and in Part II, from an independent American standpoint.

Finally, in the joint conclusions, both authors look to the future ... asking what might happen?

Brussels, St Paul and Seattle

Acknowledgements

The writing of this book would not have been possible without the cooperation and assistance of a number of friends and colleagues.

Both authors had discussions with a number of experts in fields examined in this book. Thus, André Sapir, of the European Commission and the Free University of Brussels, provided valuable insights into international monetary issues. Peter O'Brien, of Brussels, kindly agreed to discuss trade issues, as did a member of Pascal Lamy's cabinet in the European Commission. The authors are grateful to these experts for their insight.

At a particularly practical level, Ferdinando Riccardi, of the Agence Europe, Brussels graciously gave permission for the reproduction of EU trade articles in the appendices.

But, most importantly, the authors are very grateful to you, friends and relatives, who have been extraordinarily helpful. In Seattle, Jeremy Ballanger kindly procured a number of important documents and gave assistance with the preparation of the bibliography. Once again, Juan Molina, formerly of the university of St Thomas, meticulously prepared the index. Then, in a most professional manner, Peter Coffey's niece, Tracey, at the Cathedral Church of York (York Minster), with dedication and high professionalism typed the manuscript of this book.

PART ONE

The Background to the Bretton Woods System
and the International Trading System

1. The Background to and the Creation of the Original Bretton Woods System

Peter Coffey

REASONS FOR THE SYSTEM

As has already been noted, this is a particularly opportune moment to write this book since it is 60 years, almost to the day, since the creation of the original Bretton Woods system. It is therefore useful to examine the reasons for its creation, the different plans proposed, the resulting system, its experience, the 'New' system evolving in the 1970s, the changes in the 1980s, the crises of the 1990s and the creation of the World Trade Organisation (commonly known as the WTO) in the same decade.

It is particularly useful to examine the international economic situation confronting the world as the Second World War was ending and to refer to the two (but not exclusive) main plans which were proposed for the new international economic and monetary order, on which, writing in 1974,[1] the author made a number of observations. The 1930s had been notorious for a net contraction in world trade and economic development. This state of affairs had been the result of dreadfully high levels of unemployment in a number of western countries, especially in Germany, the United Kingdom and the United States. As a result of this situation, trading nations adopted a 'beggar-thy-neighbour' policy which meant that whilst they wished to continue to export their own products, they did not wish to import goods from other countries. In turn, there was a contraction in investment flows and a resulting further increase in unemployment. Consequently, the three basic aims at Bretton Woods were:

1. to create some form of credit organisation which would give temporary assistance to countries facing balance-of-payment problems;
2. to create some form of international capital agency thus averting the former erratic and destructive international capital movements, and,
3. to set up an international trade organisation which would devise and apply international trading rules.

As will be seen during the course of this work, the outcome at Bretton Woods did not exactly fulfil the expectations of the three aims as set down above. The two main plans proposed, the Keynes and White Plans (discussed in Appendix 1) for international monetary reform were quite different from each other. The outcome was a compromise which was not entirely satisfactory. Then, no international trade organisation was created. Instead, we had a treaty, the General Agreement on Tariffs and Trade (the GATT) with a small secretariat, based in Geneva, Switzerland.

THE OUTCOME: THE BRETTON WOODS SYSTEM – THE IMF AND THE IBRD (WORLD BANK)

When we talk of the Bretton Woods system we are essentially talking of an international monetary order or system, centred mainly on the IMF, which, in some way replaced the old Gold Standard system of the nineteenth century and the early part of the twentieth century. In contrast with the earlier system, the main principles of the original Bretton Woods system, until its demise in August 1971, may be listed as follows:

The IMF

The main principles, as built round the IMF were the following. First and foremost – and this was stressed by the United States – was convertibility. This stipulation and principle tended to be premature, and, in the case of Western European countries, was not achieved until the 1970s.

The second main principle was the so-called 'gold-exchange standard' whereby the United States agreed to exchange official holdings of US dollars at a rate of $35 per fine ounce of gold.

The third principle was that of exchange rate variations which were allowed when a balance of payments was in 'fundamental' disequilibrium. However, members of the Fund were expected first to have recourse to assistance from the Fund before contemplating exchange rate variations – especially devaluation.

Since countries joining the IMF made their subscriptions in two parts, 25 per cent in gold and 75 per cent in their own currencies, there was, in the early years, a constant shortage of some currencies. This problem was, to some degree, solved by increases in the IMF's funds, the creation of the Special Drawing Rights (SDR), the Standby Arrangements, the General Agreement to Borrow, the Compensation Structural Agreement and the gold facilities.

When, on 21 August 1971, the President of the United States suspended the convertibility of the US dollar into gold, the 'gold-exchange' standard ended and the monetary part of the Bretton Woods System ceased to exist. Instead, apart from continuing to help members facing balance-of-payments problems, the Fund's main activity became that of surveillance. This change also coincided with ever increasing amounts of 'hot' money which tended to severely disturb the world monetary scene.

The IBRD or the World Bank

As its original name – the International Bank for Reconstruction and Development (IBRD) – implies, the World Bank's original mission was the reconstruction of Europe. Once this was accomplished, the Bank turned its attention to the Third World. Apart from its work, one major difference between the Fund and the Bank is that only part of the Bank's capital is actually paid up. Also, unlike the Fund, the Bank consists of five separate entities. The first and most important organ is the Bank itself whose main role is to go into the world's capital markets (it has a triple A rating) and to guarantee loans to governments – usually for infrastructure projects. The maturity of these loans is usually between 15 and 20 years and there is a grace period of approximately 5 years. During the period 1992–97 the average annual loans were 15.4 billion US dollars. The second, and to most Third World countries, the more important institution, is the International Development Agency (IDA), which lends directly to governments for projects of a more social nature, such as, for example, the construction of schools, hospitals and roads. No interest is paid on these loans – only a small service charge is levied – and they have a maturity of between 35 and 40 years with a 10-year grace period. The source of the funds here are government contributions and profits from the Bank's activities. During the period 1992–97 the annual average credits were 6.1 billion US dollars. The third organ is the International Finance Association which lends directly to the private sector and which borrows 80 per cent of its funds from the markets. The last two organs, both of more recent creation, are the Multilateral Investment Guarantee Agency and the International Centre for the Settlement of Investment Disputes.

The Organisation of the Evolution of the IMF and the World Bank

By tradition, the head of the IMF is a European whilst the head of the World Bank is an American. In both cases, the Executive Board is made up of 24 executives of which 8 represent individual countries (including both France and the United Kingdom as well, of course, as the USA). The other executives represent groups of countries. Using qualified majority voting, the necessary percentage is 85 per cent. Here, the USA holds 17.87 per cent and the Eurozone countries 22.66 per cent (2000 figures). In contrast, 47 African countries hold only 4.38 per cent.

The changing roles of both organs in a changing world led to the conclusion of a rather unsatisfactory 'Concordat' in 1989. The relative lack of clarity of roles between the IMF and the World Bank, and, of course, the never-ending crises (which both authors will refer to throughout this work) led to a joint declaration on 6 September 2000. Thus, the IMF declared that its core mandate should be to promote international financial stability and macroeconomic stability and growth among the Member States as related to monetary, fiscal and exchange policies.

In contrast, the World Bank declared as its core responsibility helping countries to reduce poverty – particularly by focusing on the institutional, structural and social dimensions of development.

The World Trade Organisation (WTO)

As has already been mentioned, the World Trade Organisation (WTO), the successor to the GATT, is a relative newcomer to the international monetary, economic and trading world stage. There are similarities between the old GATT and the WTO – but there are also important differences.

Basically, both the old GATT and the WTO aim at promoting world trade through the regular organisation of international trade rounds which lead to the reduction and/or removal of tariffs and other obstacles to world trade. These trade rounds, an important subject to which we shall return, continue with the present Doha Round. There are, however, a number of basic principles which make the GATT and the WTO similar to and different from each other.

The first, and arguably the most important principle concerns equal policy treatment between members (in August 2004, there were 147 member states). This implies that if a member gives trade concessions to one other member, they must accord the same privileges to all 146 countries. The very important exception here is that based on article 24 of the old GATT Treaty which allows regional groupings. It was this exception which allowed the creation of the old European Economic Community (EEC) – now the European Union (EU) – as well as other trade groupings. However, as new members join these groups – as has just recently been the case with the EU – other members may demand compensation. The USA has constantly availed itself of this right, notably when Portugal and Spain joined the EU – and now with the 10 new members.

As with the old GATT system, members feeling harmed by the trading policies of one or some countries, may appeal to the WTO. In the case of the present organisation, the disputes go to the Dispute Settlement Panels which many Third World countries believe to be blinkered and undemocratic in nature. Once such a panel makes a decision, if the parties cannot solve their differences, then the aggrieved party may take unilateral action – this is a major difference with the GATT system.

More positively, there appears to be some hope for a continuation of the multilateral trade rounds following the agreement made in Geneva on 31 July 2004, to get the Doha Round really moving in 2005. This more positive move, which followed the major agreement by both the EU and the USA to make agricultural concessions, was a far cry from the acrimonious wrangling in Cancún, in September 2003. Much of the credit for this achievement (apart from the aforementioned concessions) must go to the G20 group of poorer countries, led by Brazil.

OVERVIEW

Without wishing to engage in repetition, it is, once again, worth stressing that the world finds itself at an important crossroads as the authors write this book. In monetary, economic and trade matters, the chief protagonists are still the EU and the USA. But despite the clear desire of both these entities to cling to their power, especially in the IMF and the World Bank, the situation is changing and must change. Without wishing to engage in the bitter and acrimonious criticism made by one writer, the present authors feel that it is, at the present time, very necessary to make constructive proposals for the reform of these vital international organisations.

NOTE

1. Peter Coffey, *The World Monetary Crisis*, Macmillan Press, London, 1974.

PART TWO

The IMF, the World Bank and the WTO:
An Independent European Assessment

2. The International Monetary Fund

Peter Coffey

INTRODUCTION

As was stressed in the introductory chapter to this book, the IMF and the World Bank, 60 years after their birth, do indeed stand at a crossroads. Thus, no time could be more opportune than the present to examine these organisations – their original roles, their record, current issues and problems and their possible future roles. In the specific case of the IMF, these tasks have reached urgent proportions, since, in March and April 2004, the Fund did itself admit, in public, that over the previous two years it had underestimated the possible upturn (in reality, a continuing downturn) in the state of the economy of Argentina. Then, at the end of July, in the same year, the Fund's own independent policy evaluation body made a scathing attack on the policy of the IMF for that same country. Such unusually open and harsh criticisms of the Fund must (without expressing a personal opinion) suggest that all is not well and that those responsible for policy analysis and the application thereof must re-examine their methods and approaches. Consequently, the time could not be more opportune for an assessment of the work of the IMF and for making constructive proposals for the future of the organisation.

THE ORIGINAL AND CHANGING ROLE OF THE IMF

Its Record

Without wishing to engage in needless repetition, it should be noted that the original (and to a large degree, continuing) role of the Fund was to help member countries facing, hopefully temporary, balance-of-payments problems. To this end, various degrees of aid have been available.[1] As, of course, a country seeks more aid, the conditions attached to the giving of such help become more rigorous. In this context, in the 1960s and the 1970s, the Fund was accused of being a 'rich man's club' because Third World countries did not seem to have access to the necessary financial aid. Subsequently, under the successive French presidents of the IMF, the aid facilities for these countries were greatly enlarged (see Appendix 1). Nevertheless, it has, at times, been the conditions attached to the aid that have raised the ire of critics. After 1971, the role of the Fund has also become that of exchange rate surveillance.

Whilst these two basic roles would seem to be both benign and relatively non-intrusive in nature, the fact that the IMF (as has been noted in the introduction) felt impelled, on 6 September 2000, to declare its core role as being a rather more progressive development one, suggests that, somewhat unofficially at least, its role, particularly in the 1980s had changed. Indeed, in his polemical work,[2] Professor Joseph Stiglitz repeatedly writes of a so-called 'Washington Consensus' whereby, under the apparent influence of the US Treasury, the IMF tried to adopt and indeed impose – for Third World countries – a policy of financial market liberalisation. This policy did not, it seems, unlike the original aims at Bretton Woods, embody any unemployment model. Furthermore, as is the case with the frequently criticised Stability Pact of the EU's Eurozone, the main drawback of any such policy option is that of 'one policy fits all'. Without wishing to repeat Professor Stiglitz's minutely detailed examples of 'interference' by the Fund in Africa, South East Asia and elsewhere, he does describe the so-called 'Washington Consensus' as being that of growth being equal to 'privatisation, liberalisation and macro-stability'. Whilst such a policy aim may (and this is questioned by critics) fit the highly developed EU Member States, it would certainly not be applicable to a number of underdeveloped Third Word countries, where, for example, the development of education must be a prime national aim. Equally, it seems that whilst structural policies do fall within the purview of the World Bank, they are not, except where ongoing and unsustainable budget deficits are a problem, the province of the IMF.

Probably of much greater concern to both friends and critics of the Fund alike is the very worrying repeated failure by the organisation's huge army of highly-educated economists to anticipate developments before they materialise. This was particularly the case for South East Asia, where, for example, in 1997, finance ministers from some of these countries were horrified at the amounts of 'hot' money flooding the area. Subsequently, they did create a regional facility, the Chiang-Mai initiative, in 2000. This is the kind of arrangement to which the author will return later in this chapter. But, what is most worrying here (as with Argentina and elsewhere) is that the Bank for International Settlements (BIS), in Basel, had, in its most reliable annual report, cast doubts (to put things mildly) on the somewhat 'rosy' picture painted by the IMF about the situation in South East Asia – to mention only the most important example. The question that must be raised, and that is indeed of great concern, therefore, is whether the economists at the BIS are better trained or more independent than their counterparts at the IMF

– this is an issue of the very greatest international importance. Should the answer (hopefully not) be that the IMF economists are less independent than those at the BIS, then we are indeed lost.

Major Current Issues

Some observers would maintain that a separate book could and should be written about current international issues. In this work, however, particularly in the present chapter, the aim is to highlight the most important issues before suggesting possible solutions. At this point, nevertheless, it is not possible to examine monetary issues separately from trade ones. To this end, a separate chapter is devoted to the World Trade Organisation (WTO). To the author, then, the most important current issues in the monetary area – and this is strictly a non-exhaustive and non-definitive list – are the following:

1. the colossal masses of so-called 'hot money' able at less than a minute's notice to shoot across the world;
2. the debt problem of many Third World countries;
3. the problem of forecasting the evolution of the economies of countries and regions;
4. the question of links between ('pegging') currencies;
5. the eternal question of the amounts of financial aid available for countries facing, hopefully temporary, balance-of-payments problems; and
6. a further point of concern for a number of observers – including the author of this chapter – is the very modest representation of Third World countries in the IMF, the World Bank and the WTO.

Some Proposals for Reform

When, in November 1998, the White House and US Congress agreed to an $18 billion funding package for the IMF, Sebastian Edwards, a professor at the UCLA's Anderson Graduate School of Management, made a call for the abolition of the IMF. His reasons for making such a revolutionary proposal were not facetious. His main reason was that the current massive flows of capital do not allow the Fund to operate effectively – particularly since it tends to react to crises after they occur. Thus, he calls for the creation of a set of small and efficient multilateral institutions. Such institutions would provide information and act quickly to enable crises to be averted.

To the author of this chapter, a major organisation already exists which does provide reliable information: and this is the BIS. Later in this chapter, we will return to the role of the BIS.

In contrast to this observation, Sebastian Edwards calls for the creation of three institutions. These bodies would be a global information agency, a contingent global financial facility, which would provide important contingent credit lines to solvent countries facing temporary balance-of-payments problems, and a kind of 'clean-up' organisation called a global restructuring agency. Thus, if these three bodies were created, logically, the IMF would be abolished.[3]

A report which has received much publicity is the Meltzer Commission Report,[4] produced under the aegis of Professor Alan Meltzer of the Carnegie-Mellon University in Pittsburgh. This report contained the following six proposals. First, it proposed that the IMF restrict lending to the short term, but only to countries in difficulties. Second, with few exceptions, loans should, nevertheless, only be made to countries meeting conditions of financial soundness. Third, the report suggests that the World Bank focus its efforts on low-income countries that lack access to capital markets. Fourth, it is proposed that regional banks should have the primary responsibility for country and regional programmes for Latin America and South East Asia. Fifth, where highly indebted poor countries 'implement an effective economic development strategy', the IMF, World Bank and regional banks should write off all claims. Sixth and finally, it was proposed that the USA should be prepared to significantly increase budgetary support for the poorest countries.

In a very critical response to the Meltzer Commission Report,[5] C. Fred Bergsten, the Director of the Institute for International Economics, in Washington DC, insisted that the report was bad policy and unfairly maligned the IMF and the World Bank. His main reasons for making such a violent counterattack were that the institutions themselves were already undertaking reforms.

More recently, in 2004, there have been calls for the creation[6] of a global currency. This call would seem to hark back to the gold standard of the nineteenth century, or perhaps to the call by Keynes for the creation of such a currency, called the 'bancor'.

SPECIAL EUROPEAN CONSIDERATIONS ABOUT MONETARY AND EXCHANGE RATE STABILITY

The Background

At most times, but, particularly since the end of the Second World War – with their vivid memories of the inflation in Germany of the 1920s and 1930s and the depression of the 1930s – Europeans have been concerned with monetary and exchange rate stability. Although in modern times this concept has been associated with Jacques Rueff of France, and, more recently, with the former

German finance minister, Theo Waigel, it does, in fact, have a rather long history – going back to the old gold standard. In the case of Jacques Rueff, his classic broadsheet, *La Réforme du Système Monétaire International*, Plon, Paris, October 1975, set the tone for official French (and, to some degree, European) monetary policy in the 1970s and 1980s, as well as current EU policy attitudes.

At the time of writing, in November and December 2004, not only the Europeans, but also the Chinese and Russians have voiced their concern about exchange rate instability, notably, the falling value of the US dollar. In fact, on 26 November 2004, the overseas service of the BBC reported that the Russian Central Bank was planning to increase the share of euros in its reserves of foreign currencies. The following day, the same service reported the same moves by China's Central Bank. It is worth noting that the decision of the European Community (EC) to create a European Monetary System (EMS) and a unit of account, the ECU, was a direct response to the American policy, backed by public statements made by US presidents, of stating their lack of concern for the value of the US dollar. Thus, the Europeans, but most notably, the Member States of the Eurozone, do prefer a state of exchange rate stability and the European Central Bank (ECB) is prepared to vary interest rates to this end.

Although, inside the EU itself and especially inside the Eurozone, the Stability Pact does ensure a degree of monetary stability and excludes excessive budgetary deficits by EU Member States, the absence of automatic fiscal transfers – as is seen in most federal states – places an extra burden on EU monetary policy.

The EU and International Exchange Rate Surveillance

As has just been observed, during the summer of 2004, some academics were, once again, airing the likelihood of creating a world currency – possibly a kind of successor to the gold standard and some sort of 'bancor' as suggested by Keynes. Since, however, the current nearest units which may be seen as an international money are the IMF's special drawing rights (SDRs) and a national currency, the US dollar, another more immediate and practical solution should be found. The author, since the first moves were made in creating a European currency, has always suggested the utilisation of a number of key national and international currencies – the US dollar, the euro, the Japanese yen and the Chinese currency – plus gold, as the key international reserve assets. Furthermore, he considers that exchange rate surveillance, which, since 1971, has been the role of the IMF, should be transferred to the BIS, which, after all, is the 'bankers' bank'. The BIS has the great advantage of being able to move quickly and discreetly, and is unlikely to incur the wrath of many countries as is the case of the IMF. There are, however, a number of solutions to the current crisis, which should be developed from a more European standpoint. It is to these that we should now turn our attention.

The Author's own Proposals for the IMF

Clearly, in view of the ongoing crises and the proposals just reviewed, change at the IMF and in the international monetary sphere is of urgent necessity. What then, should be done?

First and foremost, all critics appear to be in agreement on the need for urgent and reliable information and policy analysis. As already observed, the BIS does usually provide reliable and up-to-date information. Surely, it is not expecting too much that the IMF should have access to and be able to use this information? Also, why not 'release' those economists at the IMF who have failed in these areas, and where possible replace them, at least temporarily, by economists from the BIS whilst more permanent replacements are trained?

Then there is the strong and growing impression that the Fund is too large and unwieldy, the solution to which is that it should be split up into regional funds. Already, there is a good precedent here in the creation of the Chiang Mai facility by countries of South East Asia. Such a development could possibly also help to solve the problem of the need for a stronger representation by Third World countries. Nevertheless, it is painfully evident that the main shareholders in the Fund, the USA and the EU – with their right of veto – would probably not easily relinquish these privileges. Nonetheless, the author would suggest that the EU place, where necessary, finances at the disposal of the poorest Third World countries to enable them to increase their shareholdings. The Eurozone countries should also act more often in concert. This precise question has been recently examined by the Italian finance minister in an article in the *Journal of Common Market Studies.*[7]

The problem of the masses of 'hot' money and instant capital flows was demonstrated most vividly in September 2004, when the Citigroup, in trading of a few minutes or seconds, totally disrupted the euro bond market. Since the same financial group had also been engaged in unacceptable activities in Japan, the Japanese government forbade the group to continue activities in the country. Hence, if such practices can upset both the EU and Japan, it goes without saying that capital controls must be allowed when unwarranted, purely speculative, runs on currencies occur.

But, all this brings us to the overriding and vital question. What should the role of the IMF be – particularly in the framework of both the World Bank and the WTO?

Most importantly, it should revert to its major former role (even if split up into regional branches) of helping countries facing temporary balance-of-payments problems. The aim here is to give countries a breathing space whilst they get their houses in order.

NOTES

1. The wide range of facilities available for countries facing balance-of-payments problems include:

   (i)   standby arrangements (1952),
   (ii) compensatory financing facilities (1966) which allow up to 250 per cent of a country's quota,
   (iii) extended facilities,
   (iv) temporary oil facilities,
   (v)   special facilities for developing countries, and
   (vi) the general agreements to borrow.

2. Joseph Stiglitz, *Globalisation and its Discontents*, W.W. Norton and Company, New York and London, 2002.
3. Sebastian Edwards, 'Abolish the IMF', *Financial Times*, London, 13 November 1998.
4. International Financial Institution Advisory Commission (2000), *The Meltzer Commission Final Report*.
5. C. Fred Bergsten, 'The Empire Strikes Back', *The International Economy*, May/June 2000.
6. Notably in B. Eichengreen, R. Hausmann and U. Panizza, 'Current Mismatches, Debt Intolerance and Original Sin', NBER Working Paper 10036, 2004.
7. Lorenzo Bini Smaghi, 'A Single EU Seat in the IMF?', *Journal of Common Market Studies*, vol. 42, no. 2, June 2004. The abstract from the article is the following:

   This article examines the rationale for consolidating EU Member States' position in the International Monetary Fund (IMF). Although a substantial amount of co-ordination already takes place, particularly on issues related to the euro area and the single monetary and exchange rate policy, co-operation between EU countries in the IMF remains a relatively new phenomenon and divergences still prevail. The current institutional set-up, whereby the 15 EU countries are spread in nine constituencies, undermines effectiveness. Although there is scope for further improving co-operation, there are natural limits to what can be achieved within the existing co-operation framework. A single EU constituency would enable EU Member States to have a strong impact on IMF policies, potentially as strong as that of the US. However, this may not be an objective for all EU countries in the current conjuncture.

3. The International Bank for Reconstruction and Development: The World Bank

Peter Coffey

INTRODUCTION

The International Bank for Reconstruction and Development (IBRD), which is the other significant institution created by the Bretton Woods Agreement, was mainly intended to help in the reconstruction of post-war Europe. When this reconstruction (mainly in Western Europe) was achieved surprisingly swiftly, the institution's original raison d'être had disappeared, and, with this evolution, the name of the institution was changed to the World Bank, and its focus was redirected toward the Third World.

In the strict sense of the meaning, the World Bank is not a bank, and, furthermore, it is now composed of three institutions, the Bank itself, the International Finance Corporation (IFC), and the International Development Association (IDA). Equally, unlike 'real' banks, in the case of the World Bank, only 20 per cent of its capital is actually called up.

There is a further dual complication: first, the original long-term purpose of the Bank as seen by one of the main architects of the Bretton Woods system, Keynes, was to ensure a regular supply and movement of capital in the world to avoid a repetition of the catastrophic depression of the 1930s. Second, with the so-called 'concordat' of the 1980s between the Bank and the IMF, the real role of the World Bank has become blurred and it appears, to the author at least, that it does, on occasions, interfere in the economic and monetary policies of countries when it should not. Having made this observation, it is now useful to examine the three component parts of the institution.

In regard to the Bank itself, as we have seen, only a relatively small part of its capital has been called up, and unlike 'real' banks, it is not really in the business of making loans exclusively with its own funds. Thus, the Bank acts as a guarantor for countries which wish to enter the international capital market to raise loans. Since the Bank enjoys a triple A credit rating, the raising of such loans is a foregone conclusion. There is, however, a proviso: it would be – to put it mildly – unusual for the Bank to support a country's move into the international capital market, and the same proviso applies to a country with which the USA maintains poor or bad relations. Hence, for decades, the World Bank could not support any moves by Vietnam into the world capital markets. Here, it should be reiterated that the head of the World Bank is usually an American whereas the head of the IMF is a European.

The other component parts of the World Bank, the IFC and the IDA are very different bodies. Interestingly enough, it is perhaps the IFC that fulfils more closely one of the main original ideas of the architects of the Bretton Woods Agreement, in that, as we shall see, it lends to the private sector.

The Bank guarantees loans, which implies lending to governments. The usual maturity for such loans is between 15 and 20 years, with a grace period of 5 years. During the period 1992–97, annual average loans were $15.4 billion.

The IDA makes loans using its own funds directly to governments for socially beneficial projects such as schools, hospitals and roads. Since no interest (only a service charge) is paid on these loans, this organisation is very popular. The loans are made for periods of between 35 and 40 years, with a grace period of 10 years. The IDA funds are made up of direct contributions from governments and profits. During the period 1992–97 the annual average credits to governments were $6.1 billion. Needless to say, the demands on the resources of IDA are insatiable.

The third main organisation, the IFC, lends directly to the private sector. The finances of these loans are made up of 80 per cent from the markets and 20 per cent from the Bank itself. In 1997, it made loans totalling $8 billion.

More recently, two other bodies have been created under the aegis of the World Bank. The first of these is the Multilateral Investment Guarantee Agency. As its name implies, the Agency guarantees contracts, and, in 1997, guarantees totalling $614 million were made. The second is an International Centre for Investment Disputes.

Evolution and Problems

Unlike its European counterpart, the European Investment Bank (EIB), the World Bank is a huge organisation in terms of the numbers of persons employed. Therein lies part of its problem. According to the Meltzer Commission Report,[1] 'collectively' the World Bank Group and its three regional counterparts employ 17 000 people in 170 offices around the world, have obtained $500 billion in capital from national treasuries, hold a portfolio of $300 billion and each year extend a total of $50 billion in loans to developing countries. Furthermore, in the same Report, we read that the Bank is not (although this was one of its original official missions) alleviating poverty as much as it should, since 70 per cent of its non-aid resources flow to 11 countries that already enjoy substantial access to private resource flows. Thus, much of its work would seem to be superfluous. Equally, and as will be noted later in this chapter, the Bank (like the IMF) either because of, or despite the 'concordat' of 1989, does tend to venture into policy areas which its original mission did not envisage.

Apart from these observations, there is one major and overriding international development that has completely changed the situation underlying the original need (certainly, as Keynes saw it, as the need for some form of international investment bank) for the creation of the World Bank. This development is the huge expansion, certainly since the 1970s, of international capital flows. In many ways, the world is now awash with capital. Notwithstanding that, there never seems to be enough finance available for the socially necessary projects which are financed by organisations such as the IDA. At the same time, there is a growing need for local banks able to provide finance for small and medium-sized businesses. It is therefore, at the time of writing, particularly opportune to list all the principal problems currently facing the Bank and to make proposals for possible solutions.

Principal Problems

The main structural problem facing the World Bank is its sheer size. In an organisation of such size, problems tend to be magnified and financial wastage (armies of overpaid employees, for example) is endemic. Comparison has already been made with the EIB, whose activities (in financial terms) – both inside and outside Europe – are greater than those of the World Bank, but whose running costs are much lower. One major factor here is the more frugal lifestyle of the EIB's employees and the reliance on participating governments to co-sponsor projects.

At all times, the World Bank has been involved in huge (and sometimes ill-chosen) projects. Although one of the Bank's main officials, Miss Jessica Einhorn, director for finance, as early as 1997,[2] maintained that the organisation was cutting down on such projects, there is little evidence to suggest that this is the case.

To the author, however, one of the most worrying aspects of the World Bank's activities is its tendency to interfere (usually in cahoots with the IMF) where it should not – especially in the support of the less palatable face of capitalism. Nowhere has this pernicious tradition been more evident than in Africa, where, for example, countries in West Africa were forced to eliminate their excellent marketing boards, to the terrible detriment of the people. The outcome has been the rise of local mafias, increased poverty and a drop in economic growth. More recently, and more incredibly, the Bank forced the government of Mozambique to remove the subsidies to farmers growing cashew nuts!

Has poverty been reduced? The answer, alas, must be no. Despite the laudable aims set down in the World Bank's Development Report of September 2000–01 to reduce poverty and to encourage opportunity, empowerment and security,[3] poverty continues unabated.

One contentious area which is very dear to the hearts of most Europeans is the environment. Here, the Bank has been accused (particularly, but not exclusively, in Africa) of being financially involved with projects which are responsible for polluting the environment. This continuing problem, together with an apparent lack of energy in its support of good governance has even been highlighted, as recently as July 2004, by the Bank's own auditors,[4] as well as by outside NGOs.[5] Interestingly enough, in September 2004, in an internal Bank report, the IFC was accused of diluting the Bank's own standards on environmental controls and the policies regarding the outcome of projects with which the organisation is financially involved. In a more specific case, it is notable that the Bank and the French state electricity company (EDF), which has a majority holding (35 per cent) in the project, in September 2004, presented the plans for the hydro-electric dam, Nam Theun 2, in Laos, to understandably critical environmental groups in Paris.[6]

At a worrying financial level (as was highlighted in the Meltzer Report), the Bank, perhaps surprisingly, appears to suffer from excessive loan exposure. Historically, this has always been the danger which banks should, and, in the long run, *must* avoid.

Finally, for Europeans, it is incomprehensible that (like its sister organ, the IMF), despite the existence of regional offices in different parts of the world, the World Bank does not appear to pay much attention to the obvious rise of regionalism and the creation of regional unions (whether associations, free trade areas, customs unions or even monetary unions) throughout the world. To the author it is regionalism that offers a solution to the problems of both the IMF and the World Bank. Therefore, let us now turn to possible solutions.

Possible Solutions

In a profound and far-reaching article[7] in the *Economic Journal*, in November 1999, Joseph Stiglitz, refreshingly, emphasised the notion of the 'public good' as a quality embodied in public institutions such as the IMF and the World Bank. He also stressed the need for such institutions to show transparency and to work carefully on economic development. These would seem to be admirable principles with which to develop solutions.

In relation to the sheer size of the World Bank, without wishing to repeat Professor Meltzer's recommendations, a 'downsizing,' to use a banal business-world expression, should be the first reform. The Bank itself should be made leaner, like the EIB, and split up into regional development banks. Furthermore, except in an emergency these component parts should not make loans to rapidly developing (economically-speaking) countries.

Since capital markets have grown enormously in the past three decades, the author sees no real need for the IFC. The dissolution of this organ would also release a number of employees for other tasks or allow them to take early retirement.

In contrast, the work of IDA should, where possible, be expanded. Not only is the work of this organ socially very necessary, but it is also 'transparent'. This quality of 'transparency', which, interestingly enough, the EIB is currently emphasising,[8] should be the hallmark of both the IMF and the World Bank.

But in any solutions and reforms the European Union (EU) must play a bigger and stronger role. Despite or because of their former colonialism, many EU Member States have both longer and closer associations with Third World countries than does the United States. Equally, whilst preferential in their nature, the EU's trading policies, notably with the ACP[9] countries, are progressive in nature.

NOTES

1. International Financial Institution Advisory Commission (2000), *The Meltzer Commision Final Report*.
2. See: article: Daniel Gross, 'Brave New World Bank', *CFO*, vol. 13, no. 3, March 1997.
3. World Bank, *Development Report*, September 2000.
4. World Bank, *Annual Review of Development*, 2003, July 2004.
5. *Financial Times*, 'World Bank Faces Calls for Poverty Test on Energy Projects', 20 July 2004.
6. 'La Banque Mondiale tente de polir son image sur un barrage', *Libération*, 8 September 2004.
7. Joseph E. Stiglitz, 'The World Bank at the Millennium', *Economic Journal*, vol. 109, no. 459, November 1999.
8. Ferdinando Riccardi, 'EIB Hopes to Lead by Example on Transparency', *Bulletin Quotidien Europe*, no. 8740, 3 July 2004, Brussels.
9. African, Caribbean and Pacific.

4. The World Trade Organisation

Peter Coffey

THE BACKGROUND

Rarely in the history of the world has a new international organisation caused such animosity and agitation as has the World Trade Organisation (WTO). Created in 1995, it is the natural but rather different successor to the old GATT. Like its predecessor, it is responsible for organising 'rounds' of international trade negotiations and for the administration of a number of treaties.[1] Unlike its predecessor, the decisions of the WTO are binding. Its decisions can be appealed via its so-called 'Appellate Body', and the decisions of this institution are final and binding.

As was widely reported in even the least business, economic and trade-minded newspapers, the attempts to launch a new round of trade talks, in Seattle, in 1999, were a glorious failure. But, as will be noted in the next part of this chapter, the writing was already clearly legible on the proverbial wall, well before Seattle.

THE ORGANISATIONAL FRAMEWORK FOR THE WTO AND ITS RELATIVE SHORTCOMINGS

The major difference between the GATT and the WTO has already been noted. Put succinctly, a member state failing to obtain satisfaction vis-à-vis another member state following a complaint may take retributive action against that state.

A similarity, however, between the GATT and the WTO (the old article 24 of the GATT) is the possibility of creating regional trade groupings such as customs unions. Here, as before, members may request compensation for possible trade losses. The USA has done this vis-à-vis the EU on at least two occasions.

A major difference, nevertheless, between the GATT and the WTO is the creation in the WTO of the dispute settlement panels.

Major Problem Areas

If the writing was on the wall even before Seattle, nowhere was this more evident than in the proposed Multilateral Agreement on Investment, which, even in the opinion of the prestigious and respected French monthly journal, *Le Monde Diplomatique*, would have allowed corporations to overthrow the nation-state and democracy. It was this threat which led to the street demonstrations in Seattle and Prague.

   A concise list of the major problem areas is as follows:

1.   there appears to be a gross lack of democracy in the system;
2.   the third world countries lack influence;
3.   the dispute settlement panels seem to be exclusively concerned with their own interest, and, much more seriously, as is the case with so many lawyers, trade ones or otherwise, the panels are totally unconcerned with the consequences of their actions.

Reactions and Proposals for Solutions

In September 2000 the EU made a number of concrete proposals to attempt to solve the dilemma in which the WTO finds itself. In so doing, it was hoped that the ground would be prepared for another successful round of trade negotiations. These proposals were the following:

1.   It is both desirable and necessary to reinforce the role of the states in the WTO as well as in other international bodies.
2.   Negotiations should take place in the area of agriculture.
3.   The problem of export subsidies should be addressed.
4.   The role of competition should be enhanced but help should be given to Third World countries.

Other International Proposals after Cancún

At a more international level, and, before either the EU or the USA made substantial efforts to get the Doha Round started again – after the upheaval of the breakdown of the trade negotiations in Cancún, Mexico, in the summer of 2003 – two very important and influential bodies made a call for fairer international trade and for the opening-up of markets for Third World countries. The first report, 'A Fair Globalisation'[2] made this call without offering any real proposals for the reform of the WTO itself. A similar report, this time published by the Commonwealth Institute in London, appeared later in the same year.

Moves by the EU

Under the dynamic Irish presidency of the EU Council of Ministers in the first half of 2004 and under the equally dynamic leadership of Pascal Lamy, the EU made major moves, both in Brussels and then in the WTO Council in Geneva, to get the Doha Round moving again, and, inadvertently start the process of reforming the WTO itself. In May 2004, the Irish Prime Minister presented the critically important Common Agricultural Policy and Trade Negotiations: Irish Presidency Working Document.[3] As the title of the document implies, the aim is a further reform of the Common Agricultural Policy (CAP) – notably in the area of sugar – and, consequently, trade concessions. The other very important document (reproduced here as Appendix 3) is the Doha Development Programme Results of Negotiations at WTO General Council.[4]

The importance of this document as a trade policy negotiating blueprint cannot be overestimated. Certainly, the EU has made concessions – especially in the areas of agriculture, cotton and export subsidies. Everywhere, we read of 'special and differentiated treatment' (for Third World countries), and there appears to be a genuine desire to help the less developed countries. But, despite its great importance as a trading document, there seem to be no proposals for the reform of the WTO. In fact, in November 2004, Peter Mandelson, the successor to Pascal Lamy as EU Trade Commissioner, complained about the medieval negotiating process at the WTO and called for reform. So what should we do?

The Author's Proposals

Without wishing to repeat either the calls of NGOs or the EU for reform, the author would suggest the adoption of the five basic principles, listed below, as central to any reform of the organisation:

1. There should be a greater 'transparency' in the negotiations in the dispute settlement panels.
2. The panels themselves should be expanded to include an equal number of experts in other areas, such as, for example, the environment and social policy. The aim here would be to make clear to these trade lawyers the possible consequences of their decisions.
3. At an overall organisational level, a greater degree of flexibility, and, indeed, a streamlined approach is desirable. In a letter to the *Financial Times* in February 2001, Richard Bernal, the Jamaican Ambassador to the USA called for just such a change.[5] Thus, he suggested the creation of an intermediate body (of perhaps 25 persons) between the Director-General and the general council.

4.   A greater place and role needs to be given to Third World countries.
5.   The concept of 'vital national interest', which exists in the EU, should be
     adopted by the WTO. In this way it is hoped that the interests of member
     states will be adequately protected.

Whilst I do not for one moment imagine that the adoption of these five
principles would solve all the problems of the WTO, I believe that their
adoption would make the organisation more acceptable to the general public.
Also, it is possible that their adoption would facilitate the successful
organisation of future international trade rounds.

   In conclusion, it should be noted that for the foreseeable future, both the EU
and the USA will continue to exercise a tremendous influence in the WTO and
the organisation of future trade rounds.

NOTES

1. **The World Trade Rounds**
    One of the main, and, indeed principal and successful roles of the old GATT was the
    organisation and conclusion of world trade rounds. The main aims of such negotiations have
    been reductions in tariffs and the removal of obstacles to international trade.
        Following the Dillon Round (1960–62), the rounds at which the main protagonists were the
    old EC (now the EU) and the USA, were the Kennedy (1963–67), Tokyo (1973–79) and
    Uruguay rounds (1986–94). It is notable that with the Kennedy Round, Congress gave
    President Kennedy the right to authorise a reduction of up to 50 per cent in tariffs, to be
    agreed upon (and this is vitally important for the speedy conclusion of negotiations) by a
    specific date. In the case of the Kennedy Round, the then EEC insisted on reducing the very
    high US tariffs on certain products (for example, chemicals) before agreeing on an across the
    board reduction of 50 per cent.
        More recently, despite the European and American interest in the service sectors and the
    safeguard of investments, they have, nevertheless, reached a compromise of principle
    regarding agricultural products and export subsidies, thus allowing the latest Round – the
    Doha – to be relaunched. New agreements include the General Agreement on Trade in
    Services (GATS), the Agreement on Trade-Related Aspects of Intellectual Property Rights
    (TRIPS) and the Agreement on Trade-Related Investment Measures (TRIMS).
2. The World Commission on the Social Dimension of Globalisation (International Labour
    Organisation, Geneva), February 2004.
3. Europe Documents, no. 2370, Agence Europe, Brussels, 26 May 2004.
4. Europe Documents, no. 2376/7, Agence Europe, Brussels, 5 August 2004.
5. Letter: Review Needed of WTO Decision Process, *Financial Times*, 5 February 2001.

PART THREE

The World Bank, the IMF and the WTO:
An Independent American Assessment

5. The World Bank

Robert J. Riley

INTRODUCTION

Much like the IMF, the World Bank has come under close scrutiny over the past several decades, though more intensely so in the 1990s. Again, the criticisms come from across the political spectrum; from within academia, and from outside it. They are directed at both the scope and the particular policies of the Bank's mission: critics sometimes argue that the Bank does too much, while others claim that it does not do enough. Many believe that it focuses too heavily on market solutions, and others that it fails adequately to account for them. Jessica Einhorn (2001, p. 1), a former managing director at the Bank, writes that:

> By now, its mission has become so complex as to strain incredulity to portray the Bank as a manageable organisation. The Bank takes on challenges that lie far beyond any institution's operational capabilities. The calls for greater focus through reform seem to produce little beyond conferences and consternation, since every programme has a dedicated constituency resisting change ... whatever the remedy, it is time to redefine the bank's unwieldy mission.

She notes that the Bank has been called on to do much more than its original mission. It has been encouraged to promote development by considering and supporting market-friendly policies, and promoting a long list of 'economic goods', including stable economic environments, greater investment in human capital, stronger property rights, better-developed legal systems, promotion of sound and transparent financial markets, and paying greater attention to corporate governance. Einhorn argues that this broadening of the Bank's focus means that 'the bank is in danger of over-determining development to the point where it is a tautology ... you will be developed when you are developed' (p. 9). The solution, she argues, is to focus the Bank's energies on much more specific, narrow and targeted goals.

Calomiris (2000) concurs, defending – as a member of the Commission that produced it – the Meltzer Report (International Financial Institution Advisory Committee, 2000) in general and its particular recommendations, to be discussed below, as he argues for a clearer focus for the World Bank. He writes that:

> The Meltzer report begins with a well-defined set of economic objectives and political principles, and suggests mechanisms that would accomplish those objectives within the confines of those principles. The economic objectives of the multilateral financial institutions include: (1) improving global capital market liquidity; (2) alleviating poverty in the poorest countries; (3) promoting effective institutional reform in the legal and financial systems of developing countries that spur development; (4) providing effective global public goods, e.g., through programmes that deal with global problems of public health (particularly malaria and AIDS); (5) collecting and disseminating valuable economic data in a uniform and timely manner. The commission viewed liquidity provision during crises, macroeconomic advisory services, and data collection and dissemination to be appropriate missions of the IMF, and saw poverty alleviation, the promotion of reform, the provision of global public goods, microeconomic data collection and dissemination, and related advisory services as the central missions of the development banks. (p. 86)

Even though there might be a need for coordination of activities and policies at certain times, the Fund and the banks should pursue distinct and non-overlapping roles in his estimation.

On the other side of the debate about the Bank's scope are those who believe that the current 'mission creep' and breadth of Bank activities is just fine, or should even be expanded so that the organisation becomes a more 'holistic' kind of development agency. For example, Ardito-Barletta (1994) argues that it is appropriate and desirable that the Bank assumes responsibility for targeted lending across an even wider range of projects or activities and that it should also promote the development of stronger institutions and internal governance. He writes that:

> In the early days, bilateral development agencies paid more attention to lending for institutional framework and governance structures than did the World Bank and regional banks, which had to protect their portfolios by financing projects whose payoff was more tangible. But experience has shown that sustainable development needs a sustained policy framework. It therefore makes economic sense to introduce loans and technical assistance to build institutional and governance capacity. (p. 196)

While he acknowledges that this is a sensitive issue (as it could involve some encroachment on national sovereignty), Ardito-Barletta argues that examination and promotion of a wider range of institutional and political practices by the institution is a necessary ingredient in Bank policy.

Other experts also argue that the development banks and the IMF necessarily share many of the same concerns and – by implication – some of the same tasks, though perhaps on a more limited basis than envisioned by Ardito-Barletta. Anne Krueger (1998) – in a nice survey of the history, performance, and proposed reforms for the World Bank and the IMF – notes that:

> Both the Bank and the Fund are concerned with the economic policies pursued by individual developing countries. Experience has taught that the real returns on any investment in a country are in significant part a function of the overall macroeconomic framework within which the investment takes place. Hence, the World Bank focuses, or at least should focus, on policy issues even when undertaking project lending. And, since economic policies strongly affect growth prospects, the World Bank's Structural Adjustment lending supported changes in economic policy. Many of the same issues are, of course, also central to the Fund's lending programs. (p. 1998)

Her views support the claim that the policies and programmes of either institution have a significant impact on the efficacy and viability of the other's programmes. She notes, for example, that 'there is little point in lending to support agricultural productivity through research and extension activities ... if producer prices for agricultural commodities are depressed through domestic policies on the exchange rate' (p. 1998). Krueger goes on to argue that many of the functions of the two institutions are 'mutually complementary' and involve significant spillovers for one another. Of course, the same is likely true of the WTO – more on this later.

The survey of proposed reforms of the World Bank (and, by extension, the regional development banks) undertaken here is, as in the next chapters, by no means exhaustive. Rather, it is intended once again to provide the reader with an overview of the contours of the debate, as well as an understanding of the wide range of proposals emanating from both official and unofficial sources on both sides of the Atlantic. We begin here with the 'official views' in the United States and then move to the unofficial opinions of academics or other experts; we end this chapter with our own perspective on what the Bank should be doing differently, if anything.

OFFICIAL RECOMMENDATIONS

The Meltzer Commission Report devotes a long chapter to an assessment of the performance of the World Bank, the African Development Bank, the Asian Development Bank, and the Inter-American Development Bank; it also, of course, proposes many significant changes in their activities and functions. In short, the majority of the Commission members take the banks to task for failing to work effectively toward their stated missions, writing that 'there is a wide gap between the Banks' rhetoric and promises and their performance and achievements' (p. 52). They cite as an example the World Bank's claim that it focuses its lending in countries that are denied access to global private capital markets; in fact, 70 per cent of its loans, on average, go to eleven nations with very good access to these markets.[1]

In broad terms, the Commission believes that the Bank – like the Fund – should return to its narrower, original focus. For the former, this would mean exclusive commitment to longer-term economic development and away from its more recent emphasis on general macroeconomic policy, macroeconomic crisis management, and the so-called 'soft goals' related to social and cultural conditions (for example, the status of women). It is worth taking some space here to review in detail the main recommendations of the Commission with regard to both the development banks and the World Bank.

The Meltzer Report called for the elimination of Bank assistance – over a five-year period – to nations that have reached per capita GDP of $4000, or which have an international bonding rating of 'Baa' or higher. Further, those nations with per capita GDP above $2500 would, in their scheme, have much-reduced access to the Banks' programmes. The majority of Commission members write that 'the focus of institutional financial effort should be on the 80 to 90 poorest nations without access to private-sector resources' (p. 83). The members who signed the majority report (from here on simply called the Meltzer Report) believe that increased volumes of Bank lending to these poorer nations would induce much larger flows of *private* financial capital to them (that is, this Bank lending would enhance 'additionality'), and would force some middle-income nations (who are current Bank recipients) to pursue much-needed reforms in order to obtain greater access to private capital markets.

The Commission also recommends that the Bank provide what it labels 'poverty alleviation grants' that would subsidise services purchased by poor nations that lack private financial capital market access and which could be used to obtain appropriate public goods, including improved water supplies, vaccinations, road development and sanitation. They propose that a sliding scale of subsidy rates – inversely related to national per capita income levels – be used, with payment made directly to service providers after delivery; thus, the Bank's financial support is provided only after specified outcomes are achieved. Also, if the grants are 'used effectively' at early stages of a programme, the level of support would be increased at later stages. The Commission recommends that these grants replace traditional World Bank loans and guarantees that have in the past been used to achieve these same aims. That incentive – coupled with the recipient nation's own required matching investment into these projects – would be sufficient, they believe, to generate the commitment and discipline on the part of poor nations to make genuine progress in alleviating the worst conditions of poverty.

Along the same lines, they propose that lending policies by both the development banks and the World Bank be redesigned to foster deeper institutional reform in developing nations. In particular, they argue that a condition for new loans intended to promote institutional reform within poor nations (that lack access to private capital) should be the prior implementation of specific institutional reforms and policy changes. Under the Commission's plan, any of the Banks would ask potential borrowers to spell out a clear plan of reform – approval of a plan would serve as a necessary qualifier for a 10-year loan carrying a subsidised interest rate (the degree of interest rate subsidisation would again depend both on the country's per capita GDP and current access to international private capital markets); further, loan funds would be disbursed only after the planned set of reforms has been approved by the nation's legislative body. Also, if the nation is deemed by an independent external auditing agency to be making significant progress toward institutional reform during the original loan term, the principal repayment could be deferred for one year, up to a total of ten years. Thus, the loan period could be effectively extended to 20 years for those nations making the most significant progress with these reforms (though interest payments would not be deferred under this proposal).

Significantly, the Meltzer Commission clearly calls for an end to financial crisis lending by the Banks, with the IMF exclusively charged with this task. The Commission argues that recent involvement by the banks was 'a means for major shareholders to execute "off-balance sheet" foreign policy without submitting to the budget process in the appropriate legislative venue' (p. 88). This shift in policy would divert full use of World Bank funds toward more traditionally accepted longer-term development activities, and allow the International Monetary Fund and the banks to pursue their respective comparative advantages. In a similar vein, the Meltzer Report recommends that the Asian and Inter-American Development Agencies (this is the new name recommended for the regional development banks) assume primary responsibility for their respective regions; the World Bank (which they would rename the World Development Agency) would in turn focus its energies and resources on Africa, the Middle East, and the remaining poor nations in Europe. Both the regional agencies and the World Development Agency would seek to promote the development of transnational programmes in their assigned regions that help deliver shared, transnational public goods. The Commission writes that:

> Regional solutions that recognize the mutual concerns of interdependent nations should be emphasised. The World Development Agency should concentrate on the

production of global public goods and serve as a centralized resource for the regional agencies. Global public goods include improved treatment for tropical diseases and AIDS, rational safeguarding of environmental resources, inter-country infrastructure systems, development of tropical agricultural technology, and the creation of best managerial and regulatory practices. (p. 89)

The Commission believes that the attention paid so far by the World Bank to country or region-specific programmes (narrowly defined) has meant that it has failed to provide essential global public goods. By focusing on this more narrow mission, they believe that the volume of Bank (World Development Agency) lending would fall significantly, with the current callable capital at its disposal redeployed to the regional agencies. The new mission of the WDA would preclude investment, guarantees and lending to the private sector and instead solely consist of efforts in the public sphere. For example, they call for the elimination of the Multilateral Investment Guarantee Agency of the Bank, which provides political-risk insurance to private-sector projects.

Most provocatively (for many), the Commission majority argues that the WDA and the regional development agencies should write off – in their entirety – all claims against the 'highly indebted poor countries' if they are successful in implementing meaningful development strategies, as supervised by the agencies. They also recommend that the United States' government should significantly increase its spending on its 'effective programs to reduce poverty' (p. 91), though these are not specifically identified. The Report states that 'the current six dollars per capita currently spent [by the US] is too much for ineffective programs but not enough for effective programs' (p. 91).

The US Treasury – not surprisingly – took exception to many of these recommendations in its official response to the Meltzer Commission Report. The introduction to the Treasury response states that:

> In our view, the core recommendations of the majority [of the Meltzer Commission], taken together, would substantially harm the economic and broader national strategic interests of the United States, by reducing dramatically the capacity of the IMF and the MDBs [Multilateral Development Banks] to respond to financial crises, and by depriving them of effective instruments to promote international financial stability and market-orientated reform and development. (US Treasury, 2000, p. 5)

The US Treasury response and recommendations are broadly grounded in a belief that the international financial institutions should have neither the reduced role generally nor the much more specialised focus advocated by the Meltzer Commission. In many ways, that response is a defence of the status quo, though some suggestions for improvements are provided. We turn here to the specific objections by the Treasury to the Meltzer proposals.

The Treasury opposes the use of any rigid, strict eligibility rules for access to World Bank funds; it argued that these were neither feasible nor desirable. The Treasury report notes that under the Meltzer rules, countries including Brazil, Indonesia, Turkey and South Africa would no longer qualify for loans from the refocused development agencies. The Treasury believes that 'graduation policies designed with a fixed and excessively low threshold risk worsening economic outcomes in these countries and increasing the risk of future crises' (p. 27). These nations – and many more – do not have consistently reliable, adequate access to private capital markets and thus need continued support from both the IMF and the banks in the view of the Treasury. However, the Treasury shares the belief that Bank lending should not be provided when access to private global financial markets is available, and that graduation policies (that is, slow phase-outs of Bank support to nations as they develop) must be pursued more diligently.

The Treasury also disagrees with the Meltzer Commission regarding the relationship between the banks and the private sector, saying that the commission proposal to close both the International Finance Corporation and the Multilateral Investment Guarantee Agency, and to further eliminate Bank investments in the private sector in all forms, is ill-advised. This belief is grounded in their view that private financial capital markets are imperfect, and tend to underfund nations that are considered to be risky investments, reinforced by the Commission's claim that World Bank and development bank lending has, in fact, 'generated many times its amount in new and additional private flows' (p. 28). The Treasury thus argues strenuously for the continuation of these types of programmes. While it acknowledges that care must be taken in not merely providing cheaper capital to the private sector in recipient nations than would otherwise be provided in its absence, the Treasury believes that access for many middle- and lower- income nations has not yet been adequately deepened or stabilised, and efforts by the banks to support private-sector activities must continue until that is realised.

The Treasury also opposes the recommended elimination of World Bank financial support to nations in Latin America and Asia, as well as the proposal to transfer so-called callable capital from the World Bank to the regional development banks. The opposition to the former is based on the Treasury's perception that the World Bank has the kind of global experience and insight that can be a benefit to all regions. Its disagreement with the Commission over capital transfers from the World Bank to the regional development banks is grounded in the view that this would require a change to the charters of the institutions involved, which Treasury officials deem to be nearly impossible politically. The required changes to the charters would – in their estimation – pose tremendous legal difficulties, since the Bank has issued publicly-held bonds against its callable capital. The terms and conditions of these outstanding debt instruments would be violated should such a transfer take place.

The Treasury also goes on to recommend that the banks – and not just the IMF – should continue to provide assistance to countries experiencing financial crises, albeit only under what it calls 'exceptional circumstances'. The official Treasury position is that by helping nations under duress avoid unnecessary monetary or fiscal contractions, assisting them in efforts to restructure the financial sectors over the longer term, and working with them to reduce the negative impact on the poorest segments in society during the adjustment process, the banks can more effectively work toward their more general goals of promoting economic development. The Treasury response to the Meltzer Report notes that:

> The upsurge in multilateral development bank 'crisis' lending in the late 1990s, most of which was provided on shorter maturities and higher rates, was appropriate in the context of the acute and generalized reduction of private capital flows to emerging economies. The risks were high. However, the economic results that have emerged – in terms of helping to put in place fundamental reforms needed to restore private sector confidence – have been broadly positive. A large measure of economic and financial stability has been restored and economic growth prospects are now far better than would otherwise have been expected. (p. 31)

They also note that this 'hard-loan lending' has returned to lower, historic levels for those nations that used it during the financial crises of the 1990s, suggesting that this form of assistance is truly exceptional, and that it can play an important role in coping with macroeconomic crisis situations.

The Treasury also opposes the Meltzer Report recommendation that the banks make use of outright grants rather than loans to the poorest nations. Much of this opposition is due to the perceived political difficulties of obtaining the annual legislative approval of funding that would be required within the donor nations; it also argues that current lending practices – at highly concessional rates – generate an optimal flow of funds to the poorest nations since repayments to the banks from other borrowing nations can be recycled into new loans to the poorer nations. The Treasury also does not believe that Meltzer-style grant programmes would induce sufficient discipline and incentive on the part of poorer nations to commit to ongoing reforms and policies needed for sustained economic development.

The Treasury supports the Meltzer recommendations – at least in broad terms – that the banks should support institution-building as well as help finance the provision of global public goods, though it believes that these ought to complement rather than replace current Bank efforts. While disagreeing with the particular institutional reform programme proposed by the Commission, arguing that it would penalise many nations when they might most be in need of assistance, the Treasury concurs that greater transparency and accountability towards these ends is needed. The Treasury – at least in

2000 when it issued its response – also supports the Meltzer proposal that the US and other governments fully write-off all loans to highly-indebted poor nations; it did not, however, support a 100 per cent write-off of Bank and IMF loans to those same nations. While some write-off is desirable from their point of view, forgiveness of all loans would impose a serious burden on these institutions and induce greater moral hazard for nations that are not participants in the loan forgiveness programme.

UNOFFICIAL VIEWS

Eichengreen (2004) offers a more detailed description of some of his earlier proposals for both World Bank and International Monetary Fund reforms; these proposed reforms are one element of broader changes to the global financial system institutions and rules that he believes are needed to reduce the frequency and the severity of international financial crises. In broad terms, Eichengreen identifies currency mismatches in international lending as a real culprit in financial crises.[2] He writes that:

> Currency mismatches are widely implicated in developing countries. As noted above, developing countries that borrow abroad do so in foreign currency, virtually without exception. Countries that accumulate a net foreign debt, as capital-scarce developing countries are expected to do, therefore incur a currency mismatch. This mismatch is a source of currency instability, insofar as even limited exchange-rate depreciations significantly increase the domestic-currency cost of servicing external debts, in turn precipitating the kind of large depreciation that is the defining feature of a currency crisis. (p. 27)

He notes that one proposed solution is the introduction of a single global currency, noting that 'Europe's experience with a single currency suggests that adoption of a single currency may have positive implications for financial depth' (p. 28). A single world currency would also, naturally, eliminate the currency risk that is – in his opinion – at the heart of many financial crises. Eichengreen quickly dismisses this option as politically unrealistic. He suggests that it is instead necessary to develop the appropriate tools within the existing international framework, and in a world of very many currencies for the foreseeable future, in order to deal with the currency mismatch problem, recognising that transaction costs prevent the development of private financial market instruments toward this end. A type of market failure exists. This suggests that there is a role to be played by international organisations, including the World Bank.

Specifically, he argues that the first necessary change in this direction is the introduction of a new synthetic emerging market currency (EMC) index: he suggests that such an index could be constructed from the currencies of the twenty or so largest emerging economies, using shares of total GDP (calculated using a purchasing power parity formula) as the weights attached to each currency in the index. These nations would issue debt denominated in the local currency to the World Bank as well as to other financial institutions, with these underlying debt instruments themselves indexed to local consumer price indices (in order to discourage currency devaluations intended to reduce effective debt burdens under this new system). Eichengreen believes that this form of an EMC index would be characterised by a general trend appreciation, a fairly low degree of volatility, and would be negatively correlated with industrialised nations' consumption. All of these characteristics would make this an attractive instrument for global investors in his estimation.[3]

Eichengreen also proposes that the World Bank – along with other international financial institutions – should issue debt that is denominated in this EMC index; they could then lend (in the Bank's case, through its non-concessional window) to individual nations in local currency terms. They would in this way themselves avoid currency mismatches across their borrowing and lending operations. Eichengreen also notes that the ability to avoid currency mismatches is, currently, effectively the case for only a select number of nations, including the United States, and that this same ability needs to be extended to developing nations via this type of system. Exchange rate risk would thus be transferred away from emerging market economies and toward international investors via the Bank's new borrowing and lending practices.

He believes that this system would not induce a larger volume of Bank lending (as some might well suspect it would); it would rather generate the same benefits as that of a single global currency system and boost the growth rates of emerging market economies without a substantial increase in Bank loan volume. While he acknowledges that the Bank might face additional costs in the form of a higher risk premium on its borrowing for non-concessional lending, he believes that this will be quite small relative to the benefits generated for developing nations. Finally, Eichengreen notes that this new approach could also induce private sector use of EMC – indexed loans; this is thus an example of how the Bank can help 'complete an incomplete market'.

George Soros (2002) also weighs in on the role of the World Bank in the global economic system. He believes that the current system of loan guarantees by member nations has allowed the governments of both developed and less-developed member nations to adversely affect Bank decisions and policies – there is far less prudential lending than is optimal. He writes that:

The guarantees become instruments of control in the hands of recipient governments. The loans often serve to reinforce corrupt or repressive regimes. The governments of the developed countries that dominate the board can also exercise a nefarious influence over the lending activities of the World Bank: they can push loans that benefit their export industries or veto loans that would create competition or otherwise hurt their interests. (p. 98)

Thus, Soros supports significant changes to the operating procedures of the Bank; he argues that 'directors ought to be appointed based on their personal and professional qualifications for fixed terms and be given more independence from the governments that appoint them' (p. 104). In particular, he advocates that donor nation funds must be made without any stipulations that some of these funds be directed toward donor country interests. Further, he believes it necessary to impose term limits on the broader staff of the Bank so that their personal views and interests do not dominate policy-making; their timely return to their home nations would in turn help diffuse much-needed expertise where it would have the greatest impact. He also argues that the Bank must be more attentive to domestic political conditions within recipient nations as well as to the potential abuse of Bank funds; it should refuse to lend to 'repressive and corrupt regimes' (p. 103).

Soros takes exception to much of the Meltzer Commission findings; he – like the US Treasury in its response to the Commission report – argues against imposing a strict per capita GDP limit to qualify for Bank assistance. He is also opposed to replacing its traditional lending with outright grants, at least to the degree advocated by the Commission. He notes that middle-income nations such as Brazil or Chile (who again would be phased out of Bank assistance under the Meltzer plan) still have significant development needs that cannot be met through private capital markets alone, suggesting a much-needed continued role for the Bank. Further, increased reliance on the use of grants, he believes, would make the institution even more susceptible to donor nation pressures and politics.

Soros (2002) does not envision significant changes in Bank structure or policies at this time. He writes, with reference to his SDR (Special Drawing Rights) proposal for the International Monetary Fund (described in the next chapter) that:

> this is not the right time to embark on a major reform of the World Bank, because any restructuring is liable to result in a reduction of its resources. It would be better to implement the SDR scheme than to try to put the guarantee capital of the World Bank to more active use.

Longer-term, substantial reforms to the way the Bank conducts its business might be called for, but only after certain broader changes in the global financial system have been made.

Krueger (1998), unlike Soros, argues that a phase-out of Bank lending to middle-income nations is generally desirable;[4] she also is wary of continued project lending to lower-income nations, writing that 'if a case be made for continued Bank involvement, it is for some low-income countries, especially in Sub-Saharan Africa and South Central Asia' (p. 2007). In these cases, she notes that it is not clear that this lending will be productive given the general economic environment and policies of these impoverished nations. She notes that until these countries undertake significant and sustained overhauls of their general economic policies, Bank lending to them should be restricted to basic infrastructure development, with a suggested focus on 'education, health, development of agricultural research and extensions capabilities, and so on' (p. 2008).

In her discussion of current trends in Bank policy, Krueger argues that its increased focus on so-called 'soft target issues' (such as labour and environmental standards, women's rights, and health and safety protections) is unwise. Much like Einhorn (2001), she believes that this trend has led to a scattered approach to promoting economic development. She writes that:

> There are serious dangers with this approach. Insofar as national governments in middle-income countries are themselves unwilling to allocate sufficient resources to these 'soft issues', the question arises as to why an IFI [international financial institution] should provide financing. There is also a major danger of the Bank's embracing a wide variety of issues with little common focus, and being 'all things to all people'. (p. 2009)

She comments that much of the criticism directed at the Bank and the other IFIs is grounded in uneasiness with the kind of 'multidirectional' programming that they have pursued; this approach has also led to a potential 'overstretching' of the staff. She thus argues that 'on balance, the case for the Bank refocusing on development and shifting its efforts toward its more traditional competencies in that area for poorer countries, seems very strong' (p. 2010). She concludes her discussion with the observation that any change in the policies or approaches of the Bank (and, we presume, the other international organisations) is most likely going to emanate from within these institutions themselves. As she notes, such reform will be 'based on a process of discussion, especially by the policy community, and consensus building' (p. 2017). It is simply unrealistic to expect any single nation – including the United States – to be able to impose real changes from the outside.

The Bretton Woods Commission, chaired by former Federal Reserve chairman Paul Volcker, and composed of academic experts and eminent business leaders from around the world, issued a set of proposed reforms of the international financial institutions in 1994; the report was accompanied by a series of background papers, and it is instructive to discuss here in some detail the arguments put forth in several of these. In very broad terms, the Commission members concur that the Bank and the IMF both need to enhance market mechanisms and incentives, and to provide assistance only under more specific (and often a much narrower set of) conditions.

William Ryrie (1994), for example, claims that the emergence of neo-liberalism and the so-called Washington Consensus has solidified thinking on the central role that market forces can play in promoting more substantial economic development. The goal, he thinks, of development policies and practices should be assisting developing nations to learn to run efficient market-based economies. That implies, he believes, that the Bank and other international organisations must tailor their policies to support appropriate state activity in recipient nations. More specifically, he argues that lending by the International Finance Corporation (IFC) of the World Bank group should adhere to three principles if it is to avoid undermining market mechanisms – in fact, he notes that the IFC already abides by these in many of its lending activities. The *business principle* requires the IFC to 'be a profit-oriented institution (partly because its own profitability reflects the success of its client companies) but not a profit maximiser' (p. 109). The *catalytic principle* states that IFC funds should be used to support and encourage – though not seek to maintain control of – private market activities; thus the IFC should not be a majority stakeholder in any of the private-sector activities it supports. Its real influence, he claims, is in providing the 'seal of approval' that encourages the private capital market to support the same set of activities within recipient nations. This melds with the *additionality* principle, which states that IFC lending should only take place if private funds would not be provided in its absence, or if it supports an activity that private markets themselves would not provide.

In addition to these principles, Ryrie thinks that the IFC should observe other practices that promote the private market and economy. This might include encouraging its client companies to go public, listing themselves on national stock exchanges; investing in private companies itself; providing technical assistance to national governments in the area of securities market regulation; or helping to create local financial companies that serve to channel local funds into private investment. To accomplish these ends, the IFC, in his formulation, would increase the total volume of funds available for these purposes. He believes it unlikely that donor nations will themselves be willing to increase their contributions to the organisation. Rather, these additional loanable funds would come from the higher profits generated from its lending practices, and perhaps from a transfer of funds from the World Bank to the IFC. The transferred funds could be targeted for the development of infrastructure that meets the conditions described above.

His advice for the World Bank is that it refocus its lending efforts in a way that encourages less state-controlled and more market-oriented activity across the developing world. He argues, in fact, that excessive lending with government guarantees has hindered the development of local financial markets and thus economic development itself. The Bank must adopt a much more market-disciplined approach to project lending; this implies that lending should only support projects that will clearly not be funded by private sources, or that are by nature public goods – he cites the example of past large-scale loans to governments to help recapitalise state-owned banks as an activity the Bank should not continue (p. 108). He also suggests that the Bank should devote more of its energy and time to providing technical advice and assistance, with perhaps some of this taking the form of grants rather than loans.

Many other experts also believe that Bank reform should involve and, in turn, promote 'free market' principles. Charles Calomiris (2000), taking exception to the Treasury's response to the Meltzer Commission Report, writes that much of the criticism of that report is embedded in the erroneous belief that the operations of the IMF and the World Bank can be viewed as tools of foreign policy rather than primarily of economic policy. He argues that:

> The use of multilaterals to pursue broad foreign policy objectives forces the management of these institutions to depart from clear rules and procedures in order to accommodate ad hoc political motivations. This undermines their integrity as economic institutions, makes it hard for them to ensure their accountability, and leads to an erosion of popular support for funding the important economic goals on which they should be focused. (p. 99)

Calomiris believes that the debt burdens of quite a few of the highly-indebted nations of the world are, in fact, due to the politically-motivated nature of many of the multilateral and intergovernmental loans, which have involved less than due diligence in ascertaining that these were channelled into genuinely beneficial investment activities. He also notes that the dominance of the United States in shaping Bank and Fund lending toward foreign policy ends is likely to be eroded by the emergence of a greater number of industrialised nations as well as reinvigorated European and Japanese economies that will allow them to lay claim to a greater degree of influence in shaping multilateral policies. He writes that 'sooner or later, global economic progress will mandate the kinds of reforms our commission is recommending' (p. 101). In the end, he affirms the need to focus Bank assistance on narrower economic objectives, guided by market principles and neo-liberal ideas to the greatest possible extent.

Gustav Ranis (1994), in his contribution to the Bretton Woods Commission's background papers, argues that changes in the Bank's operations and policies ought to be geared toward making it what he called a 'better team player' vis-à-vis recipient nations as well as both private investors and donor governments. He broadly believes that the Bank has emerged as the dominant player in the area of economic development, due both to the volume of its loans to less-developed nations and to its expertise in and authority on development issues. Given these two factors, it has edged out other key players (including the regional development banks). It is – he says – in the Bank's own interest not to exert dominance but rather greater restraint in its lending, and in its leadership and expertise in development economics. Thus, he believes that the Bank should share more of its responsibility for project promotion with the regional development banks (RDBs) – it might do this by focusing its efforts more on macroeconomic analysis and programme lending, leaving other efforts to be farmed out to the RDBs. As one example, he cites the overlap between RDB and World Bank activities in the area of poverty reduction; much effort and support is duplicated or wasted in the process. He suggests that the RDBs, with their deeper knowledge of local institutions and society are better-suited for a role in providing the kind of analysis that precedes the implementation of any package of assistance; the Bank could then provide the actual funds with appropriate conditionality in place that reflects the expertise and the guidance provided by the RDBs in that first stage.

Ranis also believes that the Bank should be willing to assign responsibility for general assistance to some small countries, and perhaps sectoral efforts within certain nations, to the RDBs as well. However, this decision should only be made on a case-by-case basis rather than in a rigidly predetermined fashion. Naturally, these assignments again can be determined by the need (or lack thereof) for more localised expertise and knowledge; when done properly, such a division of labour could greatly enhance the efficiency with which the agencies help promote economic development.

Another division of labour in his formulation would involve the Bank focusing on more narrowly defined economic development issues and encouraging the United Nations to focus on the promotion of human rights, non-proliferation issues, and democratic development. He believes that the Bank's tendency to pursue 'ever-changing fads-du-jour' beyond more traditional economic objectives has led to a marked increase in volatility in Bank policy that has eroded its credibility in both developing and developed nations. To reverse this, the Bank should return to its original mission and abandon these other efforts as well as its attempts to assist with balance-of-payments crises, which – Ranis says – is an area best left to the IMF. The Bank should also seek to undertake more joint project financing with the private sector; this might involve a smaller volume of lending directed at inducing a greater degree of additionality than has been generated in the past.

He goes on to argue that even if Bank policies, assistance, and lending are focused on more narrow economic development initiatives, it is important that the Bank nevertheless better understands the broader local conditions in recipient nations. He thus proposes that it send more teams and missions into nations in order to study and understand such things as the informal sector, rural-urban divides, and so on; a more serious local presence will help the Bank better to understand the potential impact of any of its more narrowly-focused efforts. Finally, he also suggests that the Bank must have closer working relations with the GATT (now the World Trade Organisation) – the Bank has blithely made recommendations and conditions regarding both export and import policies for developing nations with insufficient attention paid to the status of multilateral trade negotiations. There is thus, he believes, much need for greater coordination between the Bank and broader trade reform efforts.[5]

OTHER CONSIDERATIONS AND AUTHOR'S PROPOSALS

As the survey above shows, proposed reforms regarding the proper scope of World Bank efforts, governance, philosophical mission, and the nuts-and-bolts of specific Bank policies and programmes run the gamut. As is the case with both the IMF and the World Trade Organisation, it is safe to say that there is widespread disagreement on these issues. The set of my own proposals might best be seen as an attempt to adjudicate these disparate views; I hope, nonetheless, that I have something unique to say in at least a few key respects.

In terms of the Bank's overall mission, we tend to concur with those experts who suggest that it should return to a narrower set of activities as envisioned in its original mission, focusing its energies and funds on the promotion of longer-term economic development. I thus believe that it should remove itself from shorter-term macroeconomic crisis management and leave that to others, notably the IMF. I do not find the argument that Bank resources can greatly enhance those of the IMF or others in the latter task convincing; if more funds are needed to support macroeconomic stabilisation efforts then they ought to be provided directly to those institutions charged with that task. The benefits from a clearly delineated division of labour are such that the Bank and the IMF (as well as other institutions) should as a general principle avoid overlap in mission. Ultimately, this view – or those to the contrary – seems to us to hinge upon the degree of economies of scale and of scope in 'manufacturing' the kinds of services and global or regional public goods in question. While much more research regarding these kinds of production effects is needed – and I encourage the Bank and others to explore the issue exhaustively – I suspect that economies of scale rather than scope hold the greatest promise for delivering the goods. More will be said about this in later chapters. Taken this as given, however, this implies that the Bank and the world economy are best served by focusing efforts on one area: longer-term economic development infrastructure as traditionally understood.

A strong case, however, can be made that all international institutions must be cognisant of trends in those conditions, institutions, and policies that are outside of their own direct purview. While this does not suggest a literal coordination of efforts across the international economic organisations, it does imply certain things for each individual organisation. More on this will be discussed in later chapters.

Let's begin with the broad mission of the Bank. Saying that it should focus its efforts on longer-term economic development is not enough; while the Bank might, as Anne Krueger (1998) suggests, be the driver of its own re-orientation,[6] I believe that it would be well-served to design strategies to promote longer-term economic development in light of the most recent work in the theory of economic development and in the provision of global public goods. Krueger writes that:

> An obvious point of departure for analysis of international financial institutions is the absence of a world government and the proposition that there may be global public goods or externalities across national boundaries. From that starting point, there could be three – not necessarily mutually exclusive – ways to proceed ... none of these approaches have been developed significantly.[7] (p. 2005)

While a consensus on these issues is not yet clear, the more recent analysis provides us with some ideas about the broad contours of Bank policies and efforts. I take some space here to consider some of the recent thinking about global public goods and general economic development.

Kaul et al. (2003) make a compelling argument that effective management of globalisation requires a greater commitment to providing global public goods – lack of progress in that direction will, they note, only contribute to greater opposition to freer trade and international efforts, to the detriment of all nations, including the United States. They also note that the stock of global public goods can be viewed as the sum of national public goods as usually defined plus 'international cooperation'. The latter can take several forms, including outward-oriented cooperation (perceived as necessary to enjoy local consumption of the good), inward-oriented cooperation (global realities require adjustment of national policies), joint intergovernmental production (activities assigned to an international organisation), and networked cooperation (adjustment of national policies geared to joining a network of other nations who have already provided for the good). The bottom line from these experts' perspective is that much deeper international coordination is needed to boost the stock of global public goods to the level required to sustain deeper globalisation into the future.

They propose a series of changes toward that end, including the designation of national lead agencies for each specific global public good, the appointment of what they call 'issue ambassadors' in each global public good area, the renaming of ministries of foreign affairs to 'ministries of foreign affairs and international relations', the establishment of 'implementation councils' for multilateral agreements, and greater involvement of 'high-level, issue-focused CEOs to lead and strategically manage public policy partnerships' (p. 52). As part of this new global public goods architecture they also advocate the creation of a new forum for public goods that is modelled on the OECD's Development Assistance Committee efforts around official development assistance.

Kaul and Le Goulven (2003) identify five basic tools that can be used to provide global public goods. These include international pooled financial incentives, incremental cost payments or compensation, global regulation, direct spending for intergovernmental activities, and user fees for the use of international services. After surveying current efforts in each of these areas, as well as discussing the appropriateness of each in sustaining different types of public goods, the authors offer three main findings. First, while the structure of public finance currently has an international dimension, the latter has not been effectively systemised (mostly, they believe, because the idea of global public goods is a relatively new one). Second, current attempts at cooperation for providing global public goods is funded through and viewed as international aid. This, they argue, blurs the fact that much of what is seen as or thought of as 'aid' can, in fact, be constructively considered enlightened self-interest; this blurring has thus led to underinvestment in global public goods. Third, there are many examples already of 'self-running' public goods, which are adequately funded through both national and private efforts. They propose that developed nations clarify the purpose of aid, and fund it independently (or distinctly) of funding for the provision of global public goods, and that they seek to identify more *national* agencies that could help provide *national* public goods that would in turn translate into global ones once a critical mass of providers at the national level are in place.

Sandler (2001) provides a nice taxonomy of the types of both international (affecting a subset of nations) and global (affecting all nations) public goods. He notes that the decision about who is to provide a public good depends critically on which type of good is in question. While he offers examples of global or international public goods that are currently provided, he does not offer possible reforms or further suggestions about which ones are currently missing and should be pursued. In order to suggest some here, it is instructive first to review his taxonomy as a useful framework for this discussion.

In determining whether a public good is an international public good (IPG) or a global public good (GPG), Sandler (2001) argues that it is important to consider the degree of rivalry, excludability, and the nature of the 'aggregation technology' through which individual (national) contributions are used as inputs into the production of the public good. With regard to the first two considerations, we have at one end pure public goods; these are fully non-rivalrous as well as non-excludable. As an example of this type he cites efforts to eliminate (or minimise) contagious diseases such as Ebola. Impure public goods are only partially non-rival and/or partially excludable in their provision – one example, he says, would be ocean fisheries in international waters; another would be missile defence systems (which are not fully excludable because of potential spillovers from a nuclear attack on any one nation).[8] So-called club goods are characterised by the full exclusion of non-club members; members pay a fee for the enjoyment of the good, and monitoring is feasible to prevent non-members from enjoying it once provided. So-called 'joint products' involve two or more public goods that may vary in their degrees of rivalry and excludability.

Beyond the kind of public good in question, another important consideration is the nature of the so-called aggregation technology that is available for the provision of the IPG or the GPG. Sandler notes that the literature has identified four broad types. The first is a simple summation technology by which individual national contributions add up to the global or international public goods – put differently, the contribution made by any one nation is a perfect substitute for that of another. A 'weakest-link' aggregation technology is one in which the level of the total IPG/GPG provision will only be as high as that afforded by the smallest contributor (or by the lowest level of provision by one nation); here he cites the example of a network that is only as effective as its least reliable part. A 'best-shot' technology is one in which the largest contribution of a single nation determines the quantity provided at the global or international level – an example would be in the area of cures for AIDS or Ebola which, once found by a 'lead nation' (which has spent the most on developing a vaccine, or perhaps is simply the luckiest), is then generally available to all other nations. A 'weighted-sum' technology is, as the name suggests, one in which the contributions by nations do not have the same proportional effect on the level of provision at the international or global level. Thus, a dollar spent by one nation does not typically make the same contribution as a dollar spent by others. The example he cites is that of acid rain prevention: given wind and climate patterns, a reduction by a polluter that is 'upwind' will have a greater impact than would a reduction in pollution by a 'downwind' contributor.

In identifying who should provide a public good – and how it should be financed – Sandler also notes that we should consider not just the aggregation technology and the degrees of rivalry and exclusion, but also the potential for economies of scope that might be achieved by a single provider. Also important is the notion of subsidiarity, which means that those most affected by spillovers of public goods should have the most say in determining their allocation and the means of funding them. As a general principle, jurisdictions should correspond to the geographic area affected by the spillover. As he notes, 'subsidiarity not only places the problem on the most appropriate participants – those with the most at stake – but it also economises on transaction costs. Focusing on the proper participants promotes allocative efficiency' (p. 25).

He then provides examples of international institutions which already provide global or international public goods across the matrix of provider-types suggested by these criteria. He notes that their existence implies that it is indeed possible to overcome free-rider problems at the international level. It is worthwhile to cite a couple of these examples here. The World Health Organisation is classified by Sandler as a provider of joint products (including the coordination of certain health programmes, medical expertise, and disease eradication and prevention); some of the public services it provides are non-excludable (for example, disease elimination) and some are not (for example, the provision of expertise).

The same idea, he argues, applies to some of the World Bank's activities, writing that:

> The World Bank is a multilateral agency that provides IPGs in terms of development assistance, technical advice, and research findings. In addition, the Bank coordinates development assistance from a host of donors including nongovernmental organizations (NGOs), countries and charitable foundations. Activities of the World Bank vary in their public characteristics and the presence of joint products. Some activities – unconditional poverty alleviation and basic research – are primarily purely public among members, while other activities – fostering environmental quality and limiting migration – are apt to have the greatest impact on host and neighboring countries. (p. 33)

Sandler argues that the assignment of voting rights based on, say, shares of total contributions toward these efforts helps to overcome free-rider problems in the provision of these public goods: institutional design is thus dependent on the type of public good, if that design is to provide nations (or other agents) with correct incentives. The bottom line is that 'the transnational community should explicitly direct scarce resources to those GPGs or IPGs that need a significant push or else a smaller coax by the transnational community. When clubs or markets can finance the IPGs, the community should sit back and let incentives guide the actions of sovereign nations' (p. 36). Identifying when that is the case, of course, is at the crux of the debate over the proper role and span of mission of the Bank, the IMF and the WTO.

P.B. Anand (2004) offers a broad review of the literature in the area of international public goods. He concurs with an earlier work by Sandler (1998) that a review of the principles of public goods provision at the international level suggests that a variety of supranational organisations should produce IPGs. He believes that the primary axes of determination of who ought to produce a particular IPG or GPG include the importance of economies of scale production (gains from locating production within a single agency) to production based on the subsidiarity principle described above (which would involve gains from decentralised production), and from specialised production concentrated on one type of public good to economies of scope via the joint production of two or more of these.[9] He suggests that further research is needed in order to make this determination in most cases. He also explores the issue of official development assistance (ODA) and the degree to which it has been used to fund GPGs and whether this is acceptable – he concludes that up to 25 per cent of ODA is diverted into the production of GPGs. This is problematic in his view since ODA is potentially highly variable (due to political pressures) and in general is subject to abuse due to a lack of accountability. This suggests that funds directly earmarked for GPG/IPG provision would be an important element in the optimal design of their production.

The World Bank itself has devoted significant energy and time to the exploration of means of achieving the Millennium Development Goals proposed by the United Nations. These include – but are not limited to – by 2015, reduction of poverty and hunger by one-half (relative to 1990 levels); achievement of universal literacy; reduction by two-thirds (compared to 1990 levels) in the under-five mortality rates; elimination of gender disparities in educational attainment at all levels; reduction by three-fourths in the maternal mortality ratio; a halt to and then reversal of the spread of HIV/AIDS, malaria and other diseases; the halving of the proportion of people without sustainable access to safe drinking water and basic sanitation; the achievement, by 2020, of a significant improvement in the lives of at least 100 million slum dwellers; development of a more rule-based, predictable, non-discriminatory trading and financial system (which would include a commitment to good governance, development, and poverty reduction – both nationally and internationally); addressing the special needs of the least developed countries (which would involve a tariff and quota-free access to export-enhanced programmes of debt relief for highly indebted poor nations and a cancellation of official bilateral debt, as well as more generous ODA for countries committed to poverty reduction).

The Bank notes that progress toward most of these goals – particularly for many African nations – has not been substantial since their publication, and it is unlikely that they will be achieved unless growth rates across the developing world are increased significantly, and very soon. To achieve this, they argue that developed nations must make substantial progress on several fronts: the elimination of remaining barriers to manufactured goods, the reduction of agricultural subsidies, the improvement of fiscal positions across many economies (notably the United States), increased direct bilateral foreign aid, and so on. In terms of its own policies, the Bank suggest that it – along with other international agencies – should work toward the implementation of the 'action plan' of the Marrakesh Roundtable on Managing for Development Results (World Bank, 2004). Several suggestions are offered in its report. First, the Bank must undertake more substantial efforts to help middle income countries (MICs):

> A key finding of this review is that despite many examples of successful Bank engagement in individual MICs, for example Brazil, China, Mexico, and Turkey, trends in Bank lending are not in line with the objective of scaling up support to MICs, given the vast number of poor people living there … going forward, the Bank is adopting a back-to-basics approach, cutting red tape by relying more on MICs' stronger policy development and systems for fiduciary and environmental safeguards, pro-actively engaging in value-adding operations in infrastructure and service delivery and promoting the use of IBRD risk-management instructions. (p. 198)

Second, the Bank concludes that it must – in tandem with other agencies – find ways to make better use of its Poverty Reduction Strategy Papers (PRSP) in the process of developing country-by-country strategies in order to make meaningful progress toward meeting the millennium goals. An important element of this, in its view, is better monitoring and appraisal of the effects of its assistance and efforts at the global and sectoral, and not just the country, level. In broad terms, however, the Bank seems convinced that the PRSP strategy will help foster country-led and thus credible strategies for economic development.

The IMF and World Bank (2004) agrees that there is substantial merit in pushing for broader, deeper use of this approach, but is more cautious in its appraisal of the successes to date. It argues that the process has been most successful in directing attention to the need for sharper focus on how to reduce poverty rather than in developing more concrete policies toward that end. It suggests that more flexible, country-specific approaches are needed, with even greater levels of input by the countries seeking assistance.

Consideration of these principles for the provision of GPGs is one piece of an analysis of the appropriate scale and scope of Bank functions. Also important in a discussion of possible reforms regarding these is an examination of some broad principles of economic development – if we are to argue that the World Bank should, say, return to its more traditional mission of promoting economic development, it is helpful to refer to some of the latest theory about economic development. I do not attempt to undertake a comprehensive survey here, but rather look again at some recent, representative work that I believe provides some guidance in thinking through potential reforms.

Recent scholarship has brought the role of geography to the forefront of development theory: distance from the equator, average daily temperature, and topography play a central role in development in this theory. This suggests that canonical policy prescriptions might have little genuine impact in promoting real economic development. Jared Diamond (1999) is a notable example of this thinking. He writes that:

> In short, only a few areas of the world developed food production independently, and they did so at widely differing times. From those nuclear areas, hunter-gatherers of some neighbouring areas learned food production, and peoples of other neighbouring areas were replaced by invading food producers from the nuclear areas ... the peoples of areas with a head start on food production thereby gained a head start on the path leading toward guns, germs and steel. The result was a long series of collisions between the haves and the have-nots of history. (p. 103)

Ecology, climate, and environment are thus pivotal determinants of current levels of economic development in Diamond's account. Put a bit differently, some people are just born lucky, and others are not, as determined – to a very significant degree – by their geographic location.

For many, this is neither palatable nor an accurate analysis of determinants of economic growth. Most scholars argue that institutional and policy reforms can indeed generate meaningful growth for all nations. Rodrik et al. (2002) explore the role played by geography, trade and institutions in economic development. In the Diamond view, geography is a primary driver of climate and natural resource ownership, which in turn affects disease control capabilities as well as institutions and all else. Since it is difficult to see how institutions and trade policy (or much else) can alter geography, the latter is considered a very deep determinant of economic development. Rodrik et al. (2002) try to estimate empirically the contribution made by each of these three in per capita real GDPs for a cross section of 80 nations. They find that 'quality of institutions trumps everything else' (p. 4). Interestingly, they find that trade integration has no significant effect on income levels while geography has at most a weak direct effect. However, each has an indirect effect on per capita real GDP through its impact on institutional development.

Noting that indicators of the quality of institutions are highly correlated, they employ an index to measure the strength of the rule of law and strength of property rights. While much of the paper is devoted to sensitivity analysis and a critique of others' work in the area, they end with a discussion of policy implications for the promotion of economic development. First, there is strong evidence that geography is not destiny, so it is possible to promote development. Second, the evidence also suggests that many of the broad market principles (strong property rights, and so on) espoused by most economists are important in development. Third, this does not tell us anything about the specific institutions that will deliver these market realities. Rodrik et al. argue that:

> Most first-order economic principles come institution-free. Economic ideas such as incentives, competition, hard-budget constraints, sound money, fiscal sustainability, and property rights do not map directly into institutional forms. Property rights can be implemented through common law, civil law, or, for that matter, Chinese-type socialism. (p. 22)

The same is true, they say, for competition, macroeconomic stability, fiscal discipline and all of the broad conditions needed for sustainable economic development. Quoting Douglass North, they note that this implies that:

> Economies that adopt the formal rules of another economy will have very different performance characteristics than the first economy because of the different informal norms and enforcement. The implication is that transferring the formal political and economic rules of successful Western economies to third-world and Eastern European economies is not a sufficient condition for good economic performance. (p. 22)

This has, of course, implications for the effective design of Bank (or IMF) policies and strategies: one size does not fit all, and we must be suspicious of a cookie-cutter approach to Bank programming.

Dani Rodrik (2003) also surveys some of the newer ideas about the types of policies that promote economic growth. He posits that much of the thinking and advice that is grounded in canonical, neoclassical economies is correct: policies that stimulate growth would thus include fiscal discipline, tax reform, privatisation, openness to foreign direct investment, deregulation, more secure property rights, reduction of corruption, independence of the central bank from the rest of government, and adherence to general WTO disciplines. Rodrik adds several less commonly accepted items to this list, including the provision of higher social safety nets, targeted poverty reduction, and what he labels 'prudent' capital-account opening (this would involve some greater degree of capital restrictions). Having identified these as the ingredients needed to foster meaningful growth, he undertakes a series of case studies of successful development strategies for several nations. He concludes that the specific institutions that might be used to support each of these are not universal; they can and should take different forms across nations. He writes that:

principles such as appropriate incentives, property rights, sound money, and fiscal solvency all come institution-free. We need to operationalise them through a set of policy actions. The experiences above show us that there may be multiple ways of packing these principles into institutional arrangements. Different packages have different costs and benefits depending on prevailing political restraints, levels of administrative competence, and market failures. The pre-existing institutional landscape will typically offer both constraints and opportunities, requiring creative shortcuts or bold experiments. From this perspective, the 'art' of reform consists of selecting appropriately from a potentially infinite menu of institutional designs. (p. 11)

Rodrik cites as one example the common recommendation that developing nations should broadly liberalise their economies; sound advice, he says, but the important issue is exactly how that is undertaken. He notes that in the case of agriculture in China, market liberalisation took place at the margins rather than in one fell swoop – the Chinese government decided to keep most of its central plan system intact, but allowed farmers to raise and produce beyond their quotas. This surplus could then be sold at market-determined prices. This strategy not only preserved an important revenue source for the government, but also introduced market incentives into an important sector of the economy – this meant that the 'income streams of initial claimants' were preserved in the transition (p. 8). Rodrik notes that this generated political support not only for this particular market liberalisation, but more broadly, allowing the Chinese government to pursue similar strategies in other sectors in the economy over time.

Vernon Ruttan (1998) surveys the evolution of growth and development theory – and the relationship between the two – since the seminal work of Harrod-Domar. As Ruttan notes, focus and energy shifted away over time from the role played by the savings rate and physical capital formation and toward the process of new technology formation in the more recent endogenous growth theory. In many of the contemporary growth models, an important element in sustaining longer-term economic development is the ability of economic agents to pursue, develop, and benefit from new ideas. Large nations have an advantage in this if 'idea formation' is subject to increasing returns to scale. The newer research also shows how smaller less-developed nations might become stuck in so-called poverty traps for long periods of time. One implication of much of this work is that less-developed, smaller nations must find policies different from those that have been pursued by (or at least currently used by) larger, more-developed countries to promote the formation of ideas and knowledge; in fact, simply adopting the specific practices (for example, regulatory frameworks) of larger nations might actually stifle economic growth and development in less-developed nations.

These papers posit that much more research is needed to explain institutional development and its effect on broader economic development. Several of the authors also argue that greater attention should be devoted to the microeconomic foundations of institutional change, and that this should inform the discussion about policies that promote that change.

Also of recent interest is the need for 'coherence' in policymaking on the part of the World Trade Organisation, the World Bank, and the IMF. This topic is covered in greater detail in the next chapter, but is worth introducing here. Many experts believe that both the Bank and the Fund must programmatically work on international trade issues to a greater degree than in the past. The World Trade Organisation (2003) itself argues that 'the IMF and the World Bank have the means to support an ambitious and successful conclusion to the Doha market access negotiations in a variety of ways' (p. 2). These efforts to assist less-developed nations would include the provision of trade policy and surveillance, help in managing the fiscal impact of tariff reductions, financial assistance for offsetting the adverse impacts from the erosion of preferential schemes that are likely from successful conclusion of the Doha Round, and help in securing more trade financing if needed. The WTO also argues that trade must be thought about to a greater degree in the Poverty Reduction Strategy Papers and Country Assistance Strategies, which are promulgated by less-developed nations with help from the IMF and the Bank. Importantly, the WTO also recommends that both institutions be given observer status in the Trade Negotiations Commission as a necessary step in helping each organisation identify ways in which it can support the work of the WTO.

The same report notes that collaborative efforts across the three institutions have already been initiated – examples cited include the IMF and World Bank Initiative for Highly Indebted Poor Countries and the Integrated Framework for Trade-Related Technical Assistance for less-developed nations; the World Bank has also recently created a Trade Department to help facilitate and explore trade issues as they relate to the work of the Bank; also noted is the 'general trend away from adjustment lending for the purpose of supporting the liberalisation of border measures, and increased use of a wider array of instruments for addressing trade issues – technical assistance and capacity building to support the public sector, and public/private sector institution building and facilitating private sector activity in trade given the central role it plays in generating export supply capacity' (p. 7).

Despite the changes in these directions, the WTO argues that the World Bank – along with donor nations themselves – needs to do more; however, in the WTO's view, the Bank's ability to deepen these efforts is constrained by two factors. First, lack of resources means that the Bank has too few funds to pursue more meaningful work on the trade agenda for less-developed nations. Second, the governments of the highly-indebted poor countries must ultimately take a lead role in formulating the exact action plans and efforts that

will effectively harness freer trade to promote real economic development –
the World Bank can help, but in many respects can play only a supporting role
in this area.

Where does all this leave us? In my view, there is little political viability in
moving the World Bank away from its primary orientation *as a bank* (by, for
example, moving toward issuing more grants). Thus, questions about the kinds
of activities that the Bank pursues can productively be thought about in the
context of research into the efficient operation of banks and financial services
more generally. Further, I am convinced by the arguments that the global
organisations can best be viewed as assisting nations at whatever level to
provide the optimal level of global and international public goods. With this in
mind, I suggest that the World Bank should stay focused on helping fund the
provision of those public goods rather than on a stable global macroeconomy
and well-functioning trade negotiations and trade dispute resolution forum.
This suggests, I believe, a greater degree of coordination of bank activities
(including lending) across nations which would more sharply focus efforts on
a narrower range of 'development purposes'. In particular, the World Bank
should make every attempt at promoting achievement of the Millennium
Development Goals discussed above.

I base this conclusion on several key assumptions, which I believe (or
hope?) are embedded in the broader literature and research. First, there seems
to be scant evidence that economies of scope in financial services and banking
are significant, while there is perhaps mixed evidence regarding the size of
economies of scale.[10] This is surely the case, I feel, across even greater
categories of services, such as assistance to supply the broadest types of global
public goods, those traditionally associated with World Bank activity, and
those not – macroeconomic stability and trade forums (that is, leave
macroeconomic stabilisation to the IMF and the provision of trade negotiation
forums to the WTO). I believe that this suggests that the Bank should pursue
a narrower rather than a wider focus – a return to its traditional mission is in
order.

Boot et al. (2002) take a theoretical approach to the question of the optimal
scale and scope for organisations; while their focus is on traditional, profit-
maximising decision-making by typical businesses (including those in the
financial services industry), their insights are suggestive for the issue here.
They find that there are certain conditions under which the expansion of
organisational scope is indeed optimal (in profit-maximisation terms) when
longer-term strategic possibilities are taken into account. However, they write
that:

> On the question of organisational boundaries, there has recently been a remarkable
> convergence of views to the theses that focus in a firm's strategic direction is

desirable and consequently the scope of its operations should be limited to what it does best. This convergence is based on the prescriptions of management strategy gurus who advocate sticking to one's knitting ... the compelling anecdotal accounts of firms that broadened their scope as well as of those that refocused, and the large-sample empirical evidence in finance that scope expansion has led to value losses on average and refocusing has improved performance. (p. 29)

This author will be the first to admit that the empirical and theoretical conclusions from the literature that focuses on canonical, profit-maximising firm behaviour must be applied with caution to the case of international organisations that are in the business of public goods provision and economic development more broadly, although I suspect that the arguments from one to the other more likely transfer than not. However, this area needs more attention, so I add to Anne Krueger's recommendation that more research be devoted to international and global public goods the recommendation that more scholarship be devoted to organisational scope, scale economies, and so on, in the case of international organisations such as the World Bank.

Of course, this could still involve an extensive menu of possible Bank activities; it is my view that a concentrated effort focused on fewer rather than many objectives would provide the greatest benefit for the funds expended. I believe that particularly promising are the priorities established by the so-called Copenhagen Consensus, an ad hoc academic forum in which development scholars debated and explored the options that countries and organisations might select in trying to promote economic development. The laundry list of action areas included civil conflicts, climate change, communicable diseases, education, financial stability, governance, hunger and malnutrition, migration, trade reform, and water and sanitation. Using cost-benefit analysis, the group broadly reached consensus on the actions they considered priorities; at the top of this list (in order) are control of HIV/AIDS, provision of micronutrients, trade liberalisation, and malaria control. At the bottom of the list were guest worker programmes for the unskilled, carbon tax systems, and the Kyoto Protocol.[11]

NOTES

1. These nations include – in order of highest to lowest share of total World Bank loans – China, Argentina, Russia, Mexico, Indonesia, Brazil, Korea, India, Thailand, Turkey, and the Philippines.
2. This is – more generally – a lucid and extremely helpful survey of competing views of international financial crises.
3. Eichengreen (2004, p. 38) believes that the low degree of volatility in the index would be at least partly due to the diversification in production across emerging economies. He writes that 'many of the countries in question are on opposite sides of the same markets. While some export oil or coffee, others import those commodities. Therefore a positive shock to

one is a negative shock to another'.

4. Krueger (1998) does, however, believe that there could be two exceptions to the no-lending rule for middle-income nations. First, in cases 'where the present set of economic policies is appalling, the availability of World Bank (and IMF programmes) could enable more rapid adaptation of economic policy reforms were a reform-minded government to come to power' (p. 2008). The second case is when expertise of the Bank can be brought to bear on policy reform in a particular sector, citing the banking industry as one example.

5. This is a recommendation that this author thinks is of particular importance. It is discussed in detail in the next chapters.

6. Krueger (1998) writes of changes in approaches and policies of these organisations that 'it is more likely that, as in the past, change will come from the international financial institutions themselves, based on a process of discussion, especially in the policy community, and consensus building' (p. 2017). She goes on to note, however, that in the case of the World Bank, it would be wise for academic economists to pursue research into alternatives to its current focus, and for the Bank genuinely to consider the conclusions of this research. Otherwise, 'the danger arises that at some future point, the current directions of the Bank will be rejected, and politicians will decide its future without a backlog of research and analysis to underpin it' (p. 2017).

7. In Krueger's (1998, p. 2005) taxonomy these include research into the incentives and gains from international cooperation, the kinds of public goods and externalities that are tied to international exchanges, and public choice theory to explain the choices and development of international institutions.

8. Sandler (2001) posits two possibilities here – one in which the good is partially excludable but non-rival, and the other in which it is fully excludable but partially non-rival. However, it seems that some public goods could be characterised by partialness along both dimensions.

9. These two axes thus carve out four quadrants and suggest four possible configurations of a GPG provider: global institution providing a narrow/specialised GPG, a single global institution providing all GPGs, regional organisations providing a specific GPG, and regional organisations providing many or all GPGs.

10. See, for example, A. Berger et al. (1993), Clark and Speaker (1994), and Huang and Wang (2004).

11. A complete description of the forum and the recommendations can be found at www.copenhagenconsensus.com.

6.   The IMF

Robert J. Riley

INTRODUCTION

The United States has much at stake in the architecture of the international economic system and the effectiveness of its primary organisations, including the International Monetary Fund. These stakes are not just economic in nature; they have very important military and political dimensions as well. American economic conditions and relations with the rest of the world influence its strategic, geopolitical decisions; the causality also goes in the opposite direction, so any discussion of economic policy should not take place in a vacuum, divorced from a broader conversation about security and political stability. As such, we cannot separate, say, our trade ties with Europe from the geopolitical alliance with our European allies. Concerned with these relationships are standards of living, domestic security and the ability to preserve our social values, all of which enter the calculus. Genuine general equilibrium thinking is needed, but is often missing from the very heated debate around narrower – albeit important – issues, such as the role of the IMF in stabilising foreign exchange rates.

In the end, the proper place and duties of the IMF and the other international organisations in the world economy depend critically, of course, on what we construe their objectives to be, as well as on our perception of the constraints they face in the global political, economic, and cultural environment. A frank assessment of these goals and parameters is thus part of the broader discussion. The nature of regional and bilateral agreements, domestic politics, and military alliances (among other factors) all impinge upon the ability of the IMF, the World Trade Organisation, and the World Bank to carry out their duties. Further, the objectives and constraints (and even our view of how they impacted the formation and effectiveness of the organisations) are likely to be quite different today than they were sixty years ago: the world and our understanding of it have changed much since 1945.

Raymond Mikesell (2000) notes that while the IMF and the other organisations have shown themselves to be remarkably adaptable to changing circumstances, they have not yet achieved the kinds of successes that had been originally envisioned. He writes that:

To a considerable degree the changes in the policies and activities of the IMF and the World Bank from those originally intended have been largely due to changes in the world financial environment that were not anticipated in 1944. The charters have not constrained their managers from doing what they wanted to do in response to the emerging world environment. In some cases they have interpreted their charters quite liberally. In other cases, they proposed amendments to the charter or requested formation of subsidiaries ... despite the flexibility of the institutions for dealing with new conditions, they have not been as successful in solving the world's major financial problems as their founders had hoped and promised to the public and their governments. (p. 406)

This suggests that a reappraisal of the structures and agendas of these institutions is very much in order. While this has been true at many points in time (if not continuously) since their creation sixty years ago, the latest set of financial crises – Mexico in 1994–95, South East Asia in 1997, and Russia in 1998 – and the subsequent withering criticism of their performances provides even greater impetus to yet another evaluation of their structures and policies in light of the most recent developments and research.

The IMF in particular has come under intense criticism over the past decade. Amongst the harshest critics is Joseph Stiglitz (2002), the former chief economist of the World Bank and Chairman of the Council of Economic Advisors under Bill Clinton (and, of course, the recipient of the 2001 Nobel Prize in Economics), who writes that:

A half century after its founding, it is clear that the IMF has failed in its mission ... many of the policies that the IMF pushed, in particular, premature capital market liberalisation, have contributed to global instability. (p. 15)

In fact, he states that the unofficial mandate of the IMF has become the preservation of the health of international banks, and not the well-being of the less developed nations to whom it often lends.[1] In his estimation, then, the Fund has abandoned, or at least woefully compromised, its core mission and raison d'être.

Stiglitz is not alone in his criticism of the organisation. These criticisms – both official and private – are many and varied. The so-called Meltzer Commission (International Financial Institution Advisory Commission, 2000) – established by the United States Congress and charged with a review of the operation of the IMF, the WTO, the World Bank, the regional development banks, and the Inter-American Development Bank (IADB) – finds fault with 'mission creep', lack of transparency, and failure to deal with international financial organisations on the part of the IMF.[2]

This same broad assessment of their performances is shared by George Soros (1998, p. 180), who writes that:

IMF programs have served to bail out the lenders and thereby encouraged them to act irresponsibly; this is a major source of instability in the international financial system. As I explained earlier, there is an asymmetry in the way that the IMF has treated lenders and borrowers. It imposed conditions on the borrowers but not on the lenders; the money it lent and the conditions that it imposed enabled the debtor countries to meet their obligations better than they would have been able to otherwise. In this indirect way the IMF was assisting the international banks and other creditors.

The criticisms of the IMF come from across the political spectrum, from 'radically' liberal to 'radically' conservative. In an essay about the role of the IMF generally and in the South East Asia crisis in particular, written for the Hoover Institute, Lawrence J. McQuillan (1998) writes that:

> The combination of tight money and high interest rates strangled East Asian economies and produced widespread insolvency. IMF policies stunted economic growth by making it extraordinarily expensive for companies and consumers to borrow and aggravated the foreign debt burden. Steven Radelet, an economist at the Harvard Institute for International Development, asks how did 'it help Thailand to deprive apparel manufacturers of the working capital needed for exports?' Alan Blinder, former vice chairman of the Federal Reserve Board and former Clinton administration economist, concedes that 'the IMF probably made the problems worse.' Steve Hanke, professor of economics at Johns Hopkins University, summarises the debacle: 'The International Monetary Fund failed to anticipate Asia's financial crisis. Then, to add insult to injury, the IMF misdiagnosed the patient's malady and prescribed the wrong medicine. Not surprisingly, the patient's condition has gone from bad to worse.' The IMF failed to recognise that the East Asian crisis was a banking crisis, not a fiscal crisis, hence, its traditional prescriptions were inappropriate and exacerbated the problem. Perhaps it is best, therefore, that governments seldom honour the terms of their loan agreements.[3]

At the other end of the political spectrum – while not in agreement with McQuillan about the specific changes in IMF practices that might be needed (as discussed below) – Paul Krugman (2003) has commented on the Fund's response to the 2001 crisis in Argentina, saying that:

> Moreover, when the economy went sour, the International Monetary Fund – which much of the world, with considerable justification, views as a branch of the US Treasury Department – was utterly unhelpful. IMF staffers have known for months, perhaps years, that the one-peso-one-dollar policy could not be sustained. And the IMF could have offered Argentina guidance on how to escape from its monetary trap, as well as political cover for Argentina's leaders, as they did what had to be done. Instead, however, IMF officials – like medieval doctors who insisted on bleeding their patients, and repeated the procedure when the bleeding made them sicker – prescribed austerity and still more austerity, right to the end. (p. 354)

Even a former Executive Director of the IMF, Jacques Polak, has offered a strong critique of the Fund's operations, writing that:

The cumulative weight of the Fund's jerry-built structure of financial provisions have meant that almost nobody outside, and indeed, few inside, the Fund understand how the organisation works, because relatively simple economic relations are buried under increasingly opaque levels of language. To cite one example, the Fund must be the only financial organisation in the world for which the balance sheet...contains no information whatsoever on the magnitude of its outstanding credits or its liquid liabilities. More seriously, the Fund's outdated financial structure has been a handicap in its financial operations.[4]

Without a doubt, there is pervasive dissatisfaction with the policies of the IMF, emanating from the 'Buchananite' public on the right to the 'Naderite' public on the left; from within the so-called establishment and from outside it; on the part of academics, captains of industry, and financiers. The only commonality across these complaints is that something is seriously broken at the IMF and had better be remedied soon.

While there has been an emergent consensus on the need for reform of the IMF, there is much less agreement about the specific remedies required, though some of the proposals perhaps share some common elements. The recommendations, much like the criticisms, run the gamut from the outright elimination of the Fund to giving it greatly enhanced powers. Some people primarily propose changes to the structure of the institution, while others suggest that changes in specific lending policies and procedures should be the focus of any reform efforts. Many individuals, of course, argue that changes to specific policies and in organisational structure are necessary. Graham and Masson (2002, p. 2) note that:

While critics agree that the system is not working well, they disagree radically on the cure. For some, particularly critics on the right like Allan Meltzer of Carnegie Mellon University, the moral hazard induced by IMF bailouts is the culprit, and any solution requires a cutback of the IMF's activities, if not its outright closure. For others who are more supportive of foreign assistance efforts, like Jeffrey Sachs of Columbia University, the problem results from the inadequacy of the resources available to the IMF to put out fires. Unlike a domestic central bank, which can pump in potentially unlimited amounts of liquidity to prevent a financial panic, the Fund cannot play the role of lender of last resort. In the middle, there are those who endorse many of the current activities of the IMF but would like to see a strengthening of the legal and institutional mechanisms to alleviate crises when they occur, for instance, through an international bankruptcy court.

This section of this chapter explores those proposals emanating from experts and authorities within the United States; it also seeks to assess the prospects and efficacy of these recommendations, and offers a synthesised view of what a reshaped IMF might look like.

Starting at one extreme of the debate, some experts have argued for the outright abolition of the IMF. In their view, the organisation was designed for an era and set of conditions at the end of World War II that were so radically different from what exists today that it is now obsolete, if not a failed experiment. Lawrence J. McQuillan (1999) writes that:

> Has the expansion of IMF financing activities alleviated the balance of payments problems of member countries and encouraged prudent, pro-growth economic policies? The evidence, much of it supplied by the IMF, demonstrates that the fund does more harm than good. Historical studies as well as recent initiatives in Mexico, East Asia, and Russia reveal that IMF financing programs, which rarely prescribe appropriate economic policies or sufficient institutional reforms, are at best ineffective and at worst incentives for imprudent investment and public policy decisions that reduce economic growth, encourage long-term IMF dependency, and create global financial chaos ...
> It is time to scrap the IMF and strengthen market-based alternatives that would promote an orderly and efficient international monetary system. Key reforms include floating exchange-rates, internationally accepted accounting and disclosure practices, unfettered private financial markets, and fundamental legal, political, and constitutional rules that would allow free markets to emerge and countries to achieve self-sustaining economic growth and development.

McQuillan is not alone. In a well-known commentary in the *Financial Times* of London, Sebastian Edwards (1998) puts the recommendation that the IMF be abolished in the very title of his column: he succinctly and without qualification states that minor reforms of the IMF are no longer enough. In his view, nothing beyond the closing of the IMF and the opening of several new global organisations in its place will suffice.[5] Other notable economists, such as Robert Barro in a *Business Week* column, have also, at least seemingly, indicated that they believe that the abolition of the Fund is amongst the possible reforms of the international financial system that might be needed. One member of the Meltzer Commission, whose report is discussed below, has also called for the abolition of the IMF.[6]

Most commentators, however, do not recommend that the Fund be closed or merged with another organisation, such as the World Bank. Rather, they propose changes in the structure, funding, and policies of the Fund. Some of these proposals come from official (that is, government) sources. Others are proffered by well-known academics; some come from individuals in finance or the private corporate sector. As I summarise what others have said about potential reforms of the IMF, I also spend some time discussing their proposals for reform of the broader international financial architecture; this is necessary because it is not possible to discuss the current or possible roles of the Fund without understanding the environment in which it operates. As one example, a return to a worldwide gold standard and pegged exchange rate regimes would likely demand something quite different of the IMF than would a universal system of genuinely floating exchange rates.

To illustrate this further, consider the proposals offered by the so-called Bretton Woods Commission, a private, independent group composed of well-known economists and former central bankers, financiers, and other experts. In a voluminous report issued in 1994, the Commission recommended that the major industrialised nations should 'strengthen their fiscal and monetary policies and achieve greater overall macroeconomic convergence ... and these countries should establish a more formal system of coordination, involving firm and credible commitments, to support these policy improvements and avoid excessive exchange rate misalignments and volatility' (p. 4). With regard to the IMF, and within that broader context, the Commission suggests that the institution should be given 'a central role in coordinating macroeconomic policies and in developing and implementing monetary reforms' (p. 5). This would involve – they say – a focus by the Fund on short-term macroeconomic stabilisation in developing economies, leaving the World Bank to deal with longer-term development issues; it would also require the advanced nations themselves to accept to a greater degree than in the past the advice of the IMF for their own conduct. In the Commission's estimation, it would also necessitate a reconfiguration of the governance structure of the organisation and the creation of a new external advisory Committee on Coordination.

Anna Schwartz (2000) seems to argue that under this 'new Bretton Woods system' the global economy would over time evolve into a system of self-sustaining exchange rates reflecting economic fundamentals, with the dollar, yen and euro serving as the lead currencies. This in turn would greatly reduce the role played by the IMF in the international financial system, whose real function was embedded in a different exchange rate system. Given other developments in global markets, including the marked increase in international capital mobility over the past several decades, she writes:

> What would there be left for the IMF to do? It could harmonise activities of national regulators. It could continue its surveillance of financial policy of member governments. It could operate as a research institution, publishing studies and statistical information.[7] (p. 24)

Thus, the part to be played by the IMF depends on the roles, functions, and policies of other major players in the world economy. This would include national central banks, regional development banks, private commercial banks, the World Bank and – as argued later – the World Trade Organisation, among others. While the focus of our discussion here will be on IMF policies and structure, we cannot avoid some broader description of the part played by these other economic agents. I now begin with proposals emanating from 'official sources', and then turn to those offered by academics, think tanks, and others. My own assessment will follow.

AMERICAN VIEWPOINTS: OFFICIAL SOURCES

In late 1998, the United States Congress established the International Financial Institution Advisory Commission, chaired by Allan Meltzer of Carnegie Mellon University, as part of legislation that authorised $18 billion of additional funding from the United States to the IMF. The Meltzer Commission (as it soon became to be known) was charged with an examination of the roles to be played by seven international financial institutions in the global economy. These seven organisations included the International Monetary Fund, the World Bank Group, the Inter-American Development Bank (IADB), the Asian Development Bank, the African Development Bank, the World Trade Organisation, and the Bank for International Settlements. The Commission issued its report in March 2000.[8] Since it recommends a wide range of changes to the functions of the IMF, a fairly lengthy review of its findings here serves as a nice organising device for a discussion of other proposals in the rest of this chapter.

The Meltzer Report is much more ambitious than many others in its call for reforms of the IMF; naturally, given the depth and breadth of changes they recommended, a wide range of experts has criticised the Commission's proposals, in terms of the broader scope as well as the details of narrower dimensions of these recommendations.

In particular, the Commission has proposed that the IMF 'be restructured as a smaller institution with three unique responsibilities' (p. 39). These would include acting 'as a quasi-lender of last resort to solvent emerging economies by providing short-term liquidity assistance to countries in need … to collect and publish financial and economic data from member countries, and disseminate those data in a timely and uniform manner … and to provide advice (but not impose conditions) relating to economic policy as part of regular "Article IV" consultations with member countries' (p. 38). Thus – except in a grave crisis that threatens broader global stability – Fund lending would be given only to pre-qualified nations. It is hoped that this would reduce the moral hazard that many (including the majority of Commission members) believe is generated by current IMF practices. Further, it would help curb if not reverse the mission creep and overlap with other organisations' missions that has occurred since 1945, and which in the Commission's view has eroded the effectiveness of the Fund in assisting nations faced with a balance-of-payments crisis.

As the Meltzer Report notes, this means that 'the IMF should be precluded from making other types of loans to member countries. The current practice of extending long-term loans in exchange for member countries' agreeing to abide by conditions set by the IMF should end' (p. 38). The Commission concludes that longer-term lending or other forms of financial assistance would best be left to the World Bank and the regional development banks. As part of this recommendation, the Meltzer Report also proposes that the Fund's Poverty and Growth Facility should be closed, which would naturally help keep the Fund focused only on the shorter-term lending directed at assisting nations in financial crisis.

The Commission also proposes a set of strict lending principles or conditions on the part of borrowing nations that must be met in order to qualify for any IMF loan. In particular, the Report states that 'every country that borrows from the IMF must publish, regularly and in a timely manner, the maturity structure of its outstanding sovereign and guaranteed debt and off-balance sheet liabilities' (p. 40). In order for all lenders properly to evaluate risks, better and more complete information is required; much of the 'imprudent' lending that has taken place, the Commission seems to say, is due to asymmetric information.

To further encourage prudent lending by banks, it is recommended that global banking regulations need to be tightened to require higher levels of capitalisation. This can be accomplished 'either by a significant equity position, in accord with international standards, or by subordinated debt held by non-governmental and unaffiliated entities' (p. 40). This will induce market-based discipline to a greater degree than exists currently. Further, 'the IMF in cooperation with the BIS (Bank for International Settlements) should promulgate new standards to ensure adequate management of liquidity by commercial banks and other financial institutions so as to reduce the frequency of crises due to the sudden withdrawal of short-term credit' (p. 8).

Regarding the macroeconomic policies on the part of nations which seek to borrow from the Fund, the Commission argues that 'the IMF should establish a proper fiscal requirement to assure that IMF resources would not be used to sustain irresponsible budget policies' (p. 40). While they note that sensible fiscal and monetary policies are perhaps more critical to economic health than is exchange rate policy, they believe that nations as a general principle should avoid adjustable peg systems; to this end, 'the IMF should use its policy consultations to recommend either firmly fixed rates (currency board, dollarisation) or fluctuating rates' (p. 43). While the exact type of system a nation decides to adopt depends on its particular circumstances it is the Commission's view – shared by many outside of the Commission – that a 'mixed' exchange rate regime increases both the likelihood and the severity of financial crises.

The Report recommends that these new rules be phased in over a three to five-year period in order to allow member nations to adjust; during the phase-in period, nations that face a financial crisis should still be allowed to borrow, albeit at penalty rate, from the Fund without having to meet the new criteria. A nation that fails to meet the new standards at any time once these are fully in place will automatically be ineligible for the lender-of-last-resort assistance provided by the Fund. Interestingly, there is no discussion of the exact sequence in which the new standards should be implemented.

The most controversial proposal by the Commission is that the 'IMF should write-off in entirety its claims against all heavily indebted poor countries (HIPCs) that implemented an effective economic development strategy in conjunction with the World Bank and the regional development institutions' (p. 9). Important ingredients in an effective development strategy – they note – are strong property rights, a healthy rule of law, and open markets.

Finally, the Commission members argue for greater transparency on the part of the IMF. This would require a series of changes in accounting practices with regard to the Fund's SDR (Special Drawing Rights) accounts and its gold transactions; more importantly, it is proposed that the Fund ought to publicise all details of its loans as well as its Article IV consultations in a timely fashion – votes of the Executive Board should be recorded and published, after a suitable period of time, alongside summaries of its meetings.

The bottom line: the Commission's recommendations would result in a leaner IMF, involved in a smaller volume of lending than is currently in place. This would require fewer resources, and would preclude any increase in the quotas paid to the Fund by member nations – the members of the Commission argue that current Fund balances would be adequate to meet its new obligations as a lender of last resort (p. 45). They propose that any need for additional funds to deal with a more general, severe global financial crisis could be handled through borrowing of convertible currencies by the Fund, to be used for very short-term liquidity loans. However, this particular need for 'more funds' would certainly be the exception to the rule.

The United States Treasury issued a response to the Meltzer Commission Report in June 2000. It believes that:

> after careful consideration of each of the recommendations in the report, we believe that, taken together, the recommendations of the majority, if implemented, would profoundly undermine the capacity of the IMF and the multilateral development banks to perform their core functions of responding effectively to financial crises and promoting durable growth and market-orientated reforms in the developing countries – and would thus weaken the international financial institutions' capacity to promote central US interests. (p. 2)

The Treasury concurs with the majority of the Meltzer Commission that the IMF should continue to play an important role in promoting global financial stability, and that there is a need for a clearer distinction between the activities of the Fund and the multilateral development banks. However, it believes that the Meltzer recommendations on the whole will not help prevent (and could contribute to) future financial crises, and would adversely affect the ability of donor nations and global organisations to encourage meaningful reform in emerging market economies. I turn here to a brief discussion of the particular objections of the Treasury to the Meltzer proposals.

The Treasury takes exception to the Meltzer recommendation that the Fund restrict its lending to only short-term liquidity assistance to nations which have met pre-qualification standards, arguing that this would severely restrict future IMF assistance to a very small subset of the nations that might require and merit it. Also, the Meltzer pre-qualification criteria focus too narrowly on financial sector conditions in the Treasury's view – it argues that many financial crises are due to a much broader set of factors. Thus, efficient Fund lending must take the entire array of conditions and factors into account. Importantly, the Treasury also thinks that this Meltzer recommendation, if enacted, would contribute to moral hazard because:

> it would provide an assurance of substantial financing, available immediately and automatically without conditions, to countries that have met the eligibility criteria but may still have fundamental macroeconomic weaknesses or structural problems in areas other than the financial sector. In our view, this approach risks creating incentives for countries to maintain inappropriate policies ... in the expectation that unconditional funds would protect them from the adverse consequences of their actions or inaction. (p. 18)

Thus, the Treasury believes that the Fund must be able to monitor and in turn condition its lending on more than just the pre-existing conditions in the financial sector of those nations requesting assistance. Conditionality as currently practised by the IMF, it is argued, is a critical factor in nudging borrowing nations to resolve macroeconomic and structural conditions that generate the need for external borrowing; it also plays an important role in monitoring the use of IMF funds to ascertain that they are spent appropriately, and in helping promote the economic conditions under which borrowing nations will be able to make good on what they have borrowed (p. 19).

The Treasury also criticises the Meltzer recommendation that Fund loans should not have a duration of more than 120 days – it points to successful past repayments by nations that have borrowed from the IMF, and notes that in even the best cases much more than four months was needed to make full repayment. Expecting nations that are in even greater financial need than these nations to make repayment in less time is not realistic. In the same way, it believes that the Meltzer proposal that borrowing nations be subject to a 'penalty rate' on Fund loans is unrealistic, as this would involve interest rates so high as to make repayment infeasible: if nations in the past have already struggled in meeting payment obligations on loans with rates up to 1700 basis points above US Treasury yields, adding a further penalty will only make matters worse.

The Treasury agrees with the Meltzer Commission that there is a real need for changes in accounting practices as well as greater transparency at the Fund itself; it also endorsed the Commission notion that the Fund's resources are adequate, at least in the short to medium term. However, it recommends – unlike Meltzer – that the Poverty Reduction and Growth Facility of the IMF remain open, though with more clearly defined duties distinct from those of the World Bank and others. The Treasury also argues against the Meltzer recommendation that OECD nations be exempt from Article IV consultations, noting that the health of these advanced economies is critical to the performance of non-OECD nations; further, it points out that several OECD nations, such as Mexico and Korea, are themselves still vulnerable to financial crises and thus stand to benefit from IMF consultations. Also, the Treasury does not endorse a full write-off of IMF loans to heavily-indebted nations, though it does agree that some substantial forgiveness is needed; it argues that the latter would help deal with the debt overhang of nations that most suffer it, without seriously exacerbating moral hazard in future Fund lending.

An important component in the Treasury's response to the Meltzer Commission Report is its reiteration of the importance of reforms to the international financial system which encourage market-based solutions to crises. It writes that:

> The IMF should continue to develop ways of catalysing market-based approaches to resolving crises, particularly where the private sector is involved, with carefully designed approaches to achieve the right balance between maximising prospects for an early recovery from the crises and the need to lessen the risk of moral hazard. (p. 11)

Thus, they argue that Fund lending should seek to foster more private financing as well as a full return to private lending after crises occur, provide a medium-term framework for debt restructuring when required, and continue to lend to nations who have suspended IMF loan repayments but are working in good faith to meet both their *private* loan obligations and Fund conditions (p. 11).

It is also worthwhile to discuss some of the IMF's own statements about its past efforts at internal reforms, as well as the hints it has provided about what the Fund might seek to do differently in the future. The IMF staff and executive board are both, of course, well aware of the many criticisms of its operations and practices. It is safe to say that none of the recommendations put forth by Fund staff members are terribly drastic; rather, they centre on refinements to its current mission and scope. However, several of these changes could by many accounts considerably enhance the efficacy of IMF programmes and development efforts. Ken Rogoff, Director of the Research Department at the IMF, responded forcefully to the Fund's most vocal critics

– and Joseph Stiglitz in particular – writing that 'many of the charges frequently levelled against the Fund reveal deep confusion regarding its policies and intentions. Other criticisms, however, do hit at potentially fundamental weak spots in current IMF practices' (p. 39). He has suggested more recently that:

> the IMF has to walk a fine line between its desire not to throw sparks on the tinder of global financial markets and its desire to defuse potential crises before it's too late. Even though our models of financial crises are far from perfect, I think that the historical experience suggests that the IMF would be moving in the right direction if it did a little less cheerleading when debts were building up and a little more whistle-blowing, to try to steer clear of the really major crises.[9]

Anne Krueger, the current Managing Director of the Fund, has outlined in several recent speeches the contours of what she labels a new Sovereign Debt Restructuring Mechanism (SDRM), which would work to more effectively restructure sovereign debt of highly-indebted nations in a financial crisis. This would bring, in her estimation, the international financial architecture and organisations up to speed with what has been a rapidly evolving environment of international financial lending.[10]

According to the IMF (2002b), the operations of the SDRM should be guided by the following principles:

- It should be used only when debt is unsustainable.
- It should involve rapid rescheduling.
- Any violation of the contract – other than the restructuring agreed upon by a majority of shareholders – must be due to problems in the resolution of the collective action mechanism.
- The design should promote greater transparency.
- It should include early and meaningful creditor participation.
- It must only be activated with the consent of the debtor nation.
- It should not be a 'detailed blueprint' of the restructuring but rather a real incentive to engage in negotiations.
- It should have a formal dispute resolution mechanism to deal with the inevitable disagreements among creditors.

Importantly, the Fund argues that its own role in an SDRM should be quite limited. The IMF report states that:

> although the SDRM would be established through an amendment of the Fund's Articles of Agreement, the SDRM should not give the existing organs of the Fund any significant legal powers. To the extent that the Fund can play a useful role in creating incentives for an appropriate use of the mechanism, these incentives should be established through the use of its existing financial and surveillance powers. In

the final analysis, however, the framework should be designed to catalyse early and effective dialogue between the debtor and creditors – it should not increase the role of the Fund in this dialogue. (IMF, 2002b, pp. 7–8)

In the IMF's plan as articulated by Krueger, the SDRM would be actualised by a new organ of the Fund – independent of the Executive Board – called the Sovereign Debt Dispute Resolution Forum (SDDRF). This would be created and charged with the power to conduct meetings between creditors and any debtor nation. These meetings would be convoked after the IMF confirmed that the debtor nation's assessment that it has an unsustainable debt burden was legitimate. The SDDRF could then authorise a temporary moratorium on debt payments. The government of the debtor nation would be asked to enact currency controls to help limit capital flight, with private borrowers in the debtor nation provided protection from any claims against them should they halt payments because of these controls.

The debtor nation and its creditors would then begin negotiations around possible designs of debt restructurings. Should an agreement be reached between the parties, the SDDRF would certify that a majority of creditors had approved a rescheduling. It could then be charged with specific enforcement powers, again agreed upon by the debtor and majority of creditors, though the exact nature of these powers is not fully specified. Thus, the SDDRF would simply serve as a facilitator of negotiations between the parties involved and would not impose its own views or policies on the negotiated settlement. The IMF report concludes that should this mechanism prove successful, the stability of the international financial system would be significantly enhanced, and creditors would be better able to assess the riskiness of any lending they undertake (p. 74).

This proposal is the most ambitious of all the Fund's recommendations regarding its own functions and policies. Several other IMF proposals, however, are worth noting here. One source for these is the series of reports issued by the Independent Evaluation Office (IEO) of the IMF, which was created by the Fund in 2001 and charged with an independent review of all Fund lending, policies and procedures. These reports offer – or will offer, as many evaluations are currently underway – several proposed changes to IMF practice, ranging from revamped conditionality requirements in fiscal, monetary or other areas, to the provision of technical assistance by the IMF to its member nations. Whether or not any of the recommendations will be implemented, of course, is not known at this time.

A November 2002 IEO report offers a series of recommended changes that may be viewed as efforts to fine-tune rather than radically overhaul existing Fund policies and strategies regarding fiscal policy conditions within borrowing nations. These reforms would include more detailed explanations by a borrowing nation of its proposed fiscal stance as well as its assumptions about economic growth. Also on the list are calls for earlier articulation by IMF reviewers of proposed changes of perceived weaknesses in borrowing nations; greater weight placed on proposed institutional changes in fiscal policymaking, and greater emphasis on explicit plans for longer-term fiscal reforms; and a clearer framework for the discussion of social issues and programmes as part of longer-term surveillance of nations that are not yet doing this as part of the Fund's poverty reduction programme.

The IEO also issued in 2003 an evaluation of the prolonged use of IMF funds, a condition that many critics argue hinders meaningful economic development for those nations that use it, as it fosters a dependency that contributes to a lack of real institutional reform. This report offers a total of fourteen recommendations regarding persistent borrowing from the Fund. Amongst the most important of these is the suggestion that differential interest rates be charged to borrowing nations, with higher rates charged for repeated borrowing from the IFM, to serve primarily as a signal to these countries that they need to re-evaluate their dependency on the Fund. Also, it is proposed that the Fund be more selective in its judgement that repeat borrowers are both able and willing to undertake their stated reforms. While any denial of further lending could exacerbate any short-term economic crisis, it could well be that this cost is more than offset by the longer-term benefits generated from meaningful fiscal reforms induced by the new IMF posture.

It is also recommended that authorities in borrowing nations should devise as part of the application process an initial draft of a real fiscal reform programme, and that this be used to undertake a meaningful open debate within their own societies in order to maximise the sense of ownership, the transparency of the process, and a deeper local understanding of the need for and benefits anticipated from these reforms. Finally, the IEO suggests that more comprehensive surveillance and detailed analysis by potential loan recipients of alternative reform processes under a range of future scenarios would significantly enhance the ability of the Fund and nations to evaluate the ongoing use of IMF monies.

NON-OFFICIAL PROPOSALS

The proposals offered by Stiglitz (2002) are grounded in his view that the global economy is prone to market failures arising from spillover effects (primarily in the form of macroeconomic transmission effects), suggesting a role for global collective action.[11] Unlike some others, Stiglitz does not seek the abolition of the IMF nor its merger with the World Bank. Given that globalisation is here to stay, he believes the need for each of these institutions to be greater than ever. However, he argues that they have to focus to a greater degree on the maintenance of full employment and less on the protection of international creditors. He also notes that many of their duties and missions overlap, suggesting a role for greater inter-organisational coordination and operation. This possibility will be taken up in the next chapter of this book, as it is a central ingredient for many who support the expansion of scope of all three of the major international organisations.

Stiglitz also proposes a change in the governance structure of the IMF through the extension of voting rights to more stakeholders (p. 226); recognising the political opposition to this proposal, and thus the likelihood that this would be years in the making, he suggests that in the interim African nations should be given speaking rights at meetings.[12] He also proposes that an independent think tank be created to provide the IMF with advice and insight. These two changes would, he thinks, provide a broader and much-needed perspective from nations outside the decision-making process on a wider range of issues around issuance of IMF loans. He believes as well that the IMF should return to its original, narrower focus on balance-of-payment crisis management, with its newly formed regional surveillance units replacing Article IV consultations by the IMF (p. 232) – these additional moves, coupled with greater transparency would in his view result in increased accountability on the part of the Fund.

Stiglitz also proposes a series of broad reforms to the international financial system, in addition to the changes he suggests for the IMF itself. These include the creation of an international bankruptcy system, at least limited restrictions on flows of so-called hot money, movement away from bailouts for nations in crisis, improved international banking regulations, higher social safety nets across the world, and what he calls improved risk management, with creditors bearing a greater share of both interest and exchange rate risk (pp. 236–40). Each of these is an important piece in providing for a more stable global financial system and world economy. This stability can be viewed as a kind of public good that will not – he says – be delivered through private markets alone. In his view, reforms of the IMF are needed because it has failed to respond adequately to what he deems to be market failures in the form of chronic international financial crises; the existence of these clearly justifies, he argues, the need for an organisation like the IMF. Thus, its abolition and simple trust in the ability of the global laissez-faire economy to deliver a stable economic environment are out of the question. Stiglitz also suggests that the reforms he proposes are important not just in more effectively delivering stability but also in promoting worldwide social justice, helping the less-developed nations finally achieve meaningful economic development.

Barry Eichengreen (2004) argues that proposals to eliminate or merge the IMF and World Bank, to create brand-new institutions, or to undertake dramatic reforms to the existing organisations are seriously misguided and are, he believes, completely unrealistic. Rather, he says, needed reforms will have to be incremental and marginal in nature.[13] Thus, he primarily proposes a series of changes in existing practice and policy rather than in the broad structure of the IMF or the international financial institutions.[14] He thinks that reforms should be centred on making certain the system is founded on what he labels four pillars: international standards for financial management and regulation, Chilean-style taxes on short-term foreign borrowing (until countries get their bank supervision functions to world-class levels), greater exchange rate flexibility for most emerging-market economies, and collective action clauses to replace large-scale IMF bailouts (p. 35).

In addition to the last proposal, Eichengreen recommends that the Fund continue to rely on surveillance of and conditionality placed on borrowing nations' broadest institutions and conditions, rather than only on monetary, fiscal and exchange rate policies and conditions. He argues that the critics of the IMF who propose that the institution narrow its focus and requirements to only these three dimensions miss an important point: the success of any policy and lending by the Fund depends on broader microeconomic and institutional realities that are intrinsically connected to fiscal, monetary, and exchange rate policies. These cannot be disentangled, and any action that is not cognisant of this will either fail or be suboptimal.

Eichengreen (2004) also proposes a more radical, though presumably what he considers a realistic, change in the governance structure of the IMF. He notes that many of the critics of the IMF argue that its decision-making and lending has become highly politicised.[15] Thus, a change in the governance structure of the Fund – which detaches lending and policy from parochial national and creditor interests only – is in order. He proposes that the Articles of Agreement be amended to augment the independence of the Executive Board and discourage the directors from taking advice from their own governments (p. 33). This would parallel, he notes, the structure of the European Central Bank. The details need to be worked out, though he suggests that multi-year terms for board members, higher compensation, and a ban on lateral career moves into government or finance for some limited period after leaving the Fund could all be part of the solution. He also argues that true Fund independence requires budgetary independence, and thus proposes that the IMF should have the ability to borrow on the international private financial market.

In order to prevent future infringements of this greater degree of independence, transparency of Fund decisions would need to be enhanced, he argues; up-and-down votes, made available to the public along with at least sketches of board discussions, would be one element of this improvement. Finally, he argues that a separate body – perhaps the International and

Financial Committee of the Fund – should be endowed with the ability to dismiss the entire board or individual directors by a super-majority vote (p. 34). This would enhance the accountability of board decisions. Eichengreen acknowledges that these changes are ambitious – impossible in some individuals' views – but achievable nonetheless.

George Soros (1998) offers a range of proposals for the broad operation of the international financial system, including greater policy coordination between the United States and Europe, limited financial capital controls, and several others that are beyond the scope of this book. He also makes recommendations that are germane to the topic at hand, and which involve more than just fine-tuning of IMF policies and practices. While he believes that the IMF has historically proven to be resilient and has tried to adapt 'valiantly' to changing conditions (p. vxi), its recent failures require the creation of a new institution to meet the realities of the modern global financial system. In particular, he proposes that an international credit insurance corporation, incorporated as part of the IMF, could help pump additional funds into the developing world at lower interest rates (via a reduction to the risk premium currently charged). He also thinks that the IMF ought to implement debt-to-equity conversion schemes as part of its programmes – this is necessary, he argues, because liquidity crises are tightly bound up with debt-to-equity ratios that are too high (p. 147). He points to the 1997 crisis in Thailand as one example of this – the IMF did not go far enough (his words) in that case by failing to insist on this kind of conversion.

In his later book, Soros (2002) proposes the formation of what he calls an SDR (Special Drawing Rights) scheme to boost the level of international assistance provided to less-developed nations. Under this plan, a special issuance of SDRs of approximately $40 billion would take place – richer nations would be committed to using their share of the newly issued SDRs for international aid as well as maintaining current levels of all other forms of assistance. Importantly, the new funds would be distributed through a new independent agency of the IMF, with term-limited directors who would determine the kinds of activities that would qualify for assistance. He argues that 'this board would propose a strategy in its annual report, but it would have no authority over the spending of funds' (p. 78). It would rather compile what he refers to as a menu of development programmes from which recipient nations could otherwise freely choose. These programmes would help provide global public goods in areas such as public health, judicial reform, information infrastructure, education and – later in the process – poverty reduction or other soft-target programmes that are currently pursued by the World Bank.

In assessing the desirability of requiring much stronger conditionality or, alternatively, much less stringent loan requirements by the Fund, Graham and Masson (2002) argue that neither is really feasible in situations such as that in

Argentina in 2001 nor, it seems, more generally. They note that Horst Köhler, former managing director of the Fund, endorsed the principle that IMF prescriptions and conditionality should not be dictated from Washington but should rather be devised and proposed by borrowing nations themselves. In this scheme as well, these nations would select a mix of policy changes (from, it is presumed, the menu of choices the IMF might offer) that they believe best fits their situation. Further, Köhler recommended that the Fund should take into account the political conditions and context within borrowing nations in order to assess the likelihood that the proposed, self-selected reforms would be implemented – the IMF could then decide whether it would lend, with the caveat that it would avoid lending to nations that are likely to make repeated requests for Fund financial assistance. Graham and Masson also note that many experts have proposed – with reference to the Argentinian case – that the Fund should demand much tougher conditions and policy reforms, in order to re-establish the credibility of both that nation and the IMF. They argue, again, that neither of these moves is desirable, writing that:

> moves toward greater selectivity and towards the exercise of political judgement on the sustainability of the government's programs are unlikely to be the right recipe – given that they would take place precisely at a time when the Argentines must resolve a crisis rooted in governance failure. Alternatively, an attempt to re-establish credibility by exacting agreement on more onerous conditions is likely to be self-defeating … More generally, the IMF cannot afford to move away from its economic focus and toward more reliance on political criteria … the international monetary system would be better served in the interim by a continued emphasis on economic criteria but a scaling back of the Fund's intrusiveness into national policymaking. (Graham and Masson, 2002, p. 3)

Thus, they also advocate a return to the original, primary, and narrower focus of the Fund.

Other experts – in line with Treasury response to the Meltzer Commission Report – staunchly support changes to IMF policy that promote and in turn rely to a greater degree on market discipline than is the current practice. Calomiris (1999) writes that:

> Economics normally provides rather dismal news – emphasising necessary tradeoffs among objectives. In the attempt to redesign financial architecture, however, such is not the case. It is not difficult to construct a set of mechanisms that concurrently resolve problems of illiquidity (by providing a responsive international lender of last resort facility alongside a domestic deposit insurance system) while avoiding the governance and incentive problems attendant to counterproductive bailouts of risk takers. *Avoiding these problems entails establishing a mechanism that ensures credible market discipline of financial institutions.* (p. 32; emphasis added)

He believes that the real challenge in instituting reform is political – none of the international organisations nor other 'vested interests' want to cede any of their current authority; of course, he says, some of them will have to if we are to achieve our objective of developing a more efficient and coherent global financial framework.

Calomiris (2000) as well as Calomiris and Meltzer (1999) specifically recommend that a 'new IMF' be created to replace the Fund and the Exchange Stabilisation Fund; this new IMF would operate as a discount window lending unit (to member nations only). Loans would be conditioned on strict adherence by borrowing nations to a set of criteria that includes a 25 per cent minimum reserve requirement for central banks of nations that peg the exchange rate, a set of tighter domestic banking regulations (the Basle standards for the most part), appropriate levels of short-term government debt, the presence of a credible and sound deposit insurance scheme, and (again, in the case of a fixed exchange rate system) domestic bank offerings of both local and foreign currencies. In addition, the financial sector must be open to foreign entry, and domestic banks must acquire a minimum percentage of their assets through the issuance of uninsured debt – this would encourage the holders of this debt to monitor and discourage excessive risk-taking on the part of banks.

The 'new' Fund's loans would have a duration of 90 days, with a single 90 day rollover allowed if a majority of members approves. Government securities (equal to 125 per cent of the value of the loan, with one-fifth composed of foreign securities) would serve as collateral, and the interest rate charged would be 200 basis points above the average yield of those government securities one week prior to the issuance of the loan. He also proposes that any nation that defaults on Fund loans would be barred from borrowing from it for five years, and then only once all arrears have been paid in full. Finally, the Fund would not impose any additional conditions other than those described above as pre-qualification criteria.

Calomiris (2000) argues that all of these ingredients must be in place; this mix of local financial sector conditions and new IMF lending policies offers the right combination of market discipline and lender-of-last resort support to help reduce the frequency and severity of financial crises. He writes that:

> The combination of domestic deposit insurance and market discipline (which prevents the abuse of deposit insurance) can resolve the threat of banking panics that result either from confusion about the incidence of shocks, or self-fulfilling concerns about the insufficiency of bank reserves. The IMF's role would be mainly to address the other liquidity problem – liquidity crises that face member governments as the result of unwarranted speculative pressure on exchange rates. This was the original intent of the IMF's founders, and it remains a legitimate objective of IMF policy. (p. 35)

In his view, the required local conditions are 'few, simple, and easily verified' and – if enacted – 'the IMF avoids the free-riding on liquidity protection and the hazard of unwittingly financing bank bailouts in the guise of liquidity protection' (p. 35). The reforms in IMF practices will keep it focused on its proper objective and help avoid mission creep and overlap with World Bank functions (which he proposes should also revert to their original design).

Calomiris and Meltzer (1999) argue that the enactment of these reforms is politically feasible if the US Congress decides that they are needed, noting that 'the US government is the largest contributor to IMF and World Bank funding. If Congress responds to public concern about the large sums spent in Mexico, Russia, Asia, and Brazil, reform could be speedy, credible, and deep' (p. 6). They also claim that these changes would greatly reduce the US Treasury's role in global financial matters, as it would remove its ability to influence the conditions under which the Fund lends to member nations, ending its ability to use its 'considerable power to push through some IMF programmes even over the objectives of senior staff and country experts within the IMF' (p. 2).

In a similar vein – though with much less in the way of detailed proposals – Feldstein (1998) argues that the Fund must return to its original focus on balance-of-payment crises and get out of the business of pushing a much broader agenda (that is, a set of many conditionality-induced reforms). He writes that:

> The IMF would be more effective in its actions and more legitimate in the eyes of emerging-market countries if it pursued the less ambitious goal of maintaining countries' access to global capital markets and international bank lending. Its experts should focus on determining whether the troubled country's problem is one of short-term liquidity and, if so, should emphasise that in its advice and assistance. It should eschew the temptation to use currency crises as an opportunity to force fundamental structural and institutional reforms in countries, however useful they may be in the long term, unless they are absolutely necessary to revive access to international funds. It should strongly resist the pressure from the United States, Japan and other major countries to make their trade and investment agenda part of the IMF funding conditions. (p. 6)

Pointing to the financial crisis in Korea in 1997, Feldstein argues that, while the structural reforms demanded of Korea by the Fund might likely enhance longer-term growth, revived access to international finance in the shorter term did not require anything more than unconditional Fund support to convince private creditors to continue their lending via a rollover of its debt. In fact, he argues, the Fund worsened the problem by creating the impression that the country would be insolvent without dramatic and far-reaching economic and institutional reforms.

Morris Goldstein (2001), in a very nice survey of proposed reforms of the international financial architecture, argues quite convincingly that serious reform by developing countries' domestic banking and financial market operations is a linchpin of broader efforts to improve the smooth operation of the global financial system. A central feature of this in his view is a significant reduction in the currency mismatches characteristic of many nations' external debts, as this seems to be a primary factor in the more serious financial crises of the 1990s. He thinks that this reduction could be achieved if the IMF demands that loan applicants provide data on existing currency mismatches in both the banking and the broader corporate sectors, an analysis of the sustainability of these mismatches, and specific remedies to reduce them. In turn, he believes that the IMF should publicise currency mismatch data in its *World Economic Outlook* or its *International Capital Markets Report* in order to provide lenders with greater information about potential risks (also encouraging greater market discipline on their part). Goldstein is also of the view that the Fund's focus should be narrowed to its traditional analysis of fiscal, monetary, and exchange rate policies, in addition to its more recent consideration of broad financial sector conditions. It should not spend time, however, on the microeconomic or other structural issues that have crept into its work over the past decade; he advocates a strict separation of duties between the World Bank (focused on the micro) and the Fund (focused on the macro), with each thus pursuing its 'comparative advantage'. Finally, he believes that smaller loan packages by the Fund – rather than interest rate differentials on IMF loans based on frequency of use or package size – hold out more promise.

In terms of broader reforms to the global financial system, he makes a strong case that developing nations should pursue either (managed) floating exchange rates or very strict pegged exchange rate systems through currency boards or dollarisation; he indicates that it is more likely that the former rather than the latter will emerge as the best (that is, least crisis-prone) policy.

This survey is by no means comprehensive; the literature is voluminous, and we can at best seek to summarise the major conclusions of some of the notable authorities and officials who have weighed in on possible reform of the IMF, in order to get a sense of the terrain and contours of proposals advanced to date. It is now time to take stock, adjudicate, and assess what the right mix of reforms is. Our assessment is premised on several fundamental assumptions.

First, like Stiglitz, I believe that international financial markets sometimes fail; like Kindleberger, that they can be subject to panics and crashes. Second, the consequences of IMF policies can impinge upon the ability of the World Bank, World Trade Organisation, and the other international institutions to execute their tasks – of course, the spillovers go in the opposite directions as well. Third, it is both in US and European interests to foster economic development in the less-developed nations of the world; this is in addition to any of the compelling arguments that it is also the morally right thing to do (something that is not the focus of this book). Fourth, any recommendations must be politically feasible – it does little good to agitate for change that is simply not possible.

Given my scepticism that markets work always and everywhere I do not endorse the elimination of the IMF; just as there is a critical need for central banks, militaries, and other agents to provide important public goods I am fully committed to the idea that there is a central role for the Fund and other international organisations to provide the public good of global macroeconomic stability. This cannot be accomplished through policy coordination alone, nor through sound economic management by individual nations, as even these are prone to unanticipated shocks. The economic stability engendered by such a global institution fosters broader geopolitical stability. As Lawrence Summers (1994, p. 424) writes:

> Historians note that democracies do not go to war with one another. Economic historians add the corollary that democracies do not survive hyperinflation. With more countries experiencing inflation rates in the hundreds and even the thousands of percent, the IMF's role is more important now than at any previous point in history.

In order to promote a stable economic and political global system, international trade organisations like the IMF (as well as the World Bank and Word Trade Organisation, as discussed in more detail in the respective chapters dealing with them) have a critical role to play; in fact, they can play an even greater role in preventing prisoners' dilemmas that arise when nations act unilaterally in setting national policies.

The question thus turns to the appropriate scope and nature of Fund policies; the proposed reforms discussed thus far (which I believe to be representative of the broad literature and debate) seem to be fairly evenly split between those that suggest an expanded, an unchanged, or a reduced role for the IMF, in terms both of the volume of lending and the breadth of conditionality placed on it. The critical issue in assessing which of these broad claims is correct seems to be the correlation between short-term and longer-term macroeconomic policies and conditions. Put differently, is it the case that a clear bifurcation of programming (a distinct separation of powers and duties) between the Fund and, say, the World Bank requires that short-term macroeconomic performance is quite independent of longer-term development strategies and conditions? Or is it the case that connections between shorter and longer-term paths of economic performance require greater coordination on the part of the international organisations that seek to shape those paths?

The Fund should certainly carefully survey exchange rate, fiscal, monetary and financial sector policies and conditions. Very few of the experts who believe there is still a role for the Fund argue that it should do away with any one of these four (though there is, of course, disagreement about the depth of analysis and conditionality along any one of these four dimensions – more on that in a moment). But what about microeconomic, political, and broader social conditions, programmes and policies – should these be part of the Fund's panoply of considerations or not? I think so, as the 'big four' dimensions are not independent of these; there is simply no way of assessing the impact of Fund conditionality in any one area without accounting for the other dimensions and the interplay across them. This is one reason why the empirical evidence on whether an interest rate hike will lead to currency depreciation or an appreciation, *ceteris paribus*, does apply. As noted by Graham Bird (2001), in discussing the crucial issue of how IMF lending and policies will affect private capital flows into less-developed nations:

> there are legitimate questions surrounding the extent to which the conventional components of conditionality, such as restrictionary fiscal and monetary policy and exchange rate devaluation, will be associated with additional capital inflows, While higher domestic interest rates may attract some forms of short-term capital, related declines in consumption and investment alongside the increased prospects of economic recession may deter portfolio investment and foreign direct investment. Sharply rising interest rates may also enhance the risks of corporate bankruptcy and expose the vulnerabilities of domestic banking and financial systems. (p. 1858)

Thus, it is not at all clear that increased interest rates will reverse the capital outflow at the root of a financial crisis – they could, in fact, worsen it. Though not the main point in the statement above, a change in interest rates could in theory lead to a change in currency value in either direction.[16] To muddy the waters still further, consider the following even more complicated scenario: investors in 1993 could have served themselves well by asking what the impact of strengthening the Mexican peso would be on the competitiveness of Mexican exports and on monetary policy, as well as on public sentiment toward broad market liberalisation, the NAFTA, and land reform policy. In turn, they could well have considered what this might imply about political stability in, say, Chiapas. Bird (2001, p. 1859) makes a similar point when he writes that:

> lending by the IMF may have a political or institutional component. There is evidence that estimating equations which contain proxies for political and institutional factors possess superior explanatory power over those which include only economic variables, suggesting that such factors exert a significant effect ... political and institutional noise surrounding Fund lending interferes with the economic signal that is being transmitted to private capital markets and either makes the catalytic effect on private capital flows weaker or more complex.

Said again, political realities affect economic conditions and the efficacy of fiscal or monetary policy; these in turn have an impact on the political landscape in very important ways. To claim that these many conditions can be readily disentangled is spurious.

This boils down to one fact: the work and the business of the Fund and the World Bank are deeply interrelated. Consider the statement of the G7 Finance Ministers of 2001, which stated that:

> The IMF and World Bank have different mandates and need to respect them. Nevertheless, the issues they deal with are increasingly interrelated and in some countries their activities are interdependent. In this respect, they should continue to work closely together to improve efficiency and exchange of information. This would require a clearer definition of their respective responsibilities and activities, and continued development of more effective mechanisms of cooperation. (p. 35)

On the other hand, as noted in the previous chapter on the World Bank, there seems to be credible evidence that economies of scale trump economies of scope for financial services and other organisations. As noted, it seems likely that expansion of scope carries with it substantial risks in terms of loss of effective focus and attainment of objectives. Again, this evidence is not conclusive and more research is needed before we can claim that the matter is settled. However, it seems sufficiently suggestive to make the case that the IMF should keep a narrow focus on macroeconomic financial crisis management while the World Bank maintains its focus on promotion of longer-term economic development.

How do we reconcile these competing pressures on organisational functions and policies? It seems that the implication is that an optimal equilibrium (that is, configuration of organisational duties) is one that has each organisation focusing on the provision of one *type* of lending but with each allowed to incorporate any set of factors – including those that are perhaps more directly germane to the lending of the other – into its calculation of rate of return. This would enter via the size of the risk premium that might be charged, based on the expected probability of default generated by the full set of conditions and possible outcomes. Of course, this implies that each institution must be careful that it is not imposing cross-conditionality vis-à-vis the lending requirements of the other; this can be ascertained through the sharing of 'formulas' employed by each organisation in making a determination regarding its own focused lending. This is not to say that either the Fund or the World Bank must charge the full rate or risk premium in all cases; however, neither can totally disregard the prospects for repayment of loans and must thus incorporate these kinds of calculations in appropriate ways.

NOTES

1. Stiglitz (2002, p. 209) states that 'while misguidingly working to preserve what it saw as the sanctity of the credit contract, the IMF was willing to tear apart the even more important social contract. In the end, it was the IMF policies which undermined the market as well as the long-run stability of the economy and society.' He also argues that IMF policies have encouraged the flow of hot money, which has helped accelerate the transmission of contagion effects, due to the moral hazard problem of IMF lending coupled with the conditionality of IMF loans that leads to downturns that impinge on imports from trading partners.
2. International Financial Institutions Advisory Commission (2000), *The Meltzer Commission Final Report*.
3. The essay is available at http://www.hoover.stanford.edu/publications/epp/98/98b.html.
4. As quoted in the Meltzer Report, p. 34.
5. In particular, Edwards (1998) recommends that the USA, Britain and Japan convene a new international meeting on international financial architecture to set up three new agencies. These would include what he calls a Global Information Agency, Contingent Global Financial Facility, and the Global Restructuring Agency. The first of these would certify the basic health of nations; the second would provide liquidity-crunch lending to certified nations; the third would act as an international bankruptcy agency that would help crisis nations through an international Chapter 11 process.
6. In his dissenting opinion in the Report, Dr Lee Hoskins writes that 'The best solution to international financial crisis is to allow markets to work their will. Intervention by the IMF or other crisis manager creates moral hazard, leads to less efficient financial markets and supports the continuation of bad economic policies in many countries around the world. A true world liquidity crisis, were it to occur, can only be dealt with by central banks since they are the source of base money. In short, I believe the United States and the world would be better off without the IMF' (p. 110).
7. In fact, Schwartz concludes that 'a new Bretton Woods system is not needed so long as independent central banks worldwide set as their primary goal an inflation free economy, as is indeed the case in the advanced industrialised nation' (p. 25). Presumably, this would create a stable financial system and, in my estimation, greatly reduce the role of the IMF as well.
8. The Committee voted 8–3 in support of the final report; a dissenting report was also issued that explained on which recommendations the minority disagreed with the rest of the Commission. This is discussed further below.
9. Kenneth Rogoff (2003b).
10. As Krueger (2002b) notes, over the past several decades, deeper integration of financial markets, issuance of debt across more legal jurisdictions, greater use of securities and less of bank loans, and heterogeneity across debt instrument characteristics all combine to create a serious need for more orderly debt reschedules.
11. Stiglitz notes that Keynes, who he calls the intellectual grandfather of the IMF, was cognisant of this in his promotion of the Bretton Woods institutions, providing a coherent theory of the public good nature of much international macroeconomic policy.
12. Other writers also think that less-developed nations need a stronger voice in Fund decision-making; the proposed mechanism by which this is to be achieved varies. Askari (2004) believes it unlikely that these countries will be given a greater percentage of voting rights or some other radically different representation. Rather, they must work within existing frameworks to have their positions taken more seriously. He writes that 'it is futile to expect a radical change in the governance of the IMF ... Industrial countries will continue to dominate the agenda and policies ... Although the underlying voting power influences the outcomes, the "voice" of participants in policy debates in the decision-making bodies, namely the Executive Boards, is often more effective than the votes. Developing countries could develop common positions, based on their agreed collective interests, and press them in the two executive boards' (p. 61).

13. Eichengreen (2004) notes that this has been the nature of all changes in the international monetary system, with the exception of the more discontinuous and radical creation of the Bretton Woods system itself. The propensity for slow change is grounded in the network nature of the global financial system.
14. Eichengreen is seconded on this point by Charles Kindleberger (2000, p. 124), who writes that 'small improvements in the forehandedness and transparency of the IMF countries, in present lines of policy, fiscally and monetarily for the latter, are more promising' than far-reaching new designs.
15. Interestingly, Eichengreen (2004) does not clearly state whether he agrees that in actuality the Fund has become highly politicised, or whether the public's impression that it has is sufficient to motivate his proposed changes.
16. For additional discussion of the empirical evidence regarding interest rate changes and currency values see Radelet and Sachs (1998).

7. The World Trade Organisation

Robert J. Riley

INTRODUCTION

In many respects, academic criticism of the World Trade Organisation is much less intense than that of either the World Bank or the International Monetary Fund. Anne Krueger (1998), in her discussion of the evolution of Bank and Fund policies, writes that:

> In pondering these issues, one striking fact should be borne in mind: the most effective institution over the past half century – judged by world economic performance – was the GATT, which was not even an international organisation. The WTO came about, almost without planning, because it was in the interests of the major trading nations to strengthen the organisation. (p. 2017)

John Jackson (1994) also argues that the GATT has been tremendously successful, and proposes some of the reasons behind its record since it was founded. He writes that:

> Despite this inauspicious beginning, the GATT has been remarkably successful over its nearly five decades of existence. Its success is partly due to its ingenious and pragmatic leadership, particularly in its early years, as the GATT struggled to fill the gap left by the failure of the International Trade Organisation. (p. 134)

He argues that while the GATT suffered from many early problems and 'birth defects', including ineffective dispute resolution mechanisms, it has managed to evolve and improve over the past 50 years. He finds the creation of the WTO, with the establishment of that mechanism in particular, to be yet another step forward in its institutional development.

In a similar vein, Charnovitz (2002) makes the case that many of the current challenges and criticisms that the GATT/WTO now faces are in fact due to its tremendous successes and accomplishments. Again because of its track record, many more advocates of different causes or agendas 'want into' the forum in order to achieve their own ends. As he writes:

> The vigorous debate about the WTO's purview demonstrates the vitality of the organisation. Governments and private actors are not clamouring to broaden the

charter of most other international institutions. The WTO has become a magnet for expansionist ideas because it is perceived as powerful and effective. (p. 29)

He notes, of course, that while situating more issues within the WTO would be a positive development for many, it would be a disturbing move for others who believe that this would only further help the WTO effectively promote a globalisation agenda that has adverse consequences for much of the world.

One dissenting voice about the performance of the GATT/WTO in obtaining meaningful trade liberalisation is that of Andrew Rose. In a series of recent papers he has explored the degree to which the organisation has contributed to increased trade volumes and more liberal trade policies. Rose (2003) examines the impact that the OECD, the IMF and the WTO have on bilateral trade flows, and finds that OECD membership has a significant positive impact on the volume of nations' overall trade; he concludes, on the other hand, that membership in the WTO has not contributed to a significant degree to bilateral trade flows.[1]

The question of efficacy of the GATT and WTO in expanding global trade is, however, far from settled. Recent work by Subramanian and Wei (2004) claims that the organisation has had a significant, positive impact on international trade. They write that:

Our paper shows, however, that the GATT/WTO has done a splendid job of promoting trade wherever it was designed to do so and correspondingly failed to promote trade where the design of rules militated against it. The WTO has served to increase industrial country imports substantially, possibly by about 68 percent, the result of successive rounds of tariff liberalisation. (p. 20)

While they find that the GATT/WTO had much less impact on the import volumes of developing nations, they conclude that a significant increase in global trade has been due to the efforts of the organisation and the series of trade liberalisation rounds it has supported. This is – it seems – the consensus of the broader economics profession.

Stiglitz (2002) devotes just a few pages to the performance of the WTO, arguing only that it must work more strenuously to take into account the interests of developing nations, though he finds the Doha Round of talks to be a step in the right direction; Soros (1998) mentions the WTO only once, and that is in a discussion of market reforms on the part of China. The Meltzer Commission – likely because of its general mandate – gives the WTO only one page in its final report.

Of course, while there is broad agreement in the academy about the successes of the WTO (and the GATT before it), there is much less consensus regarding the proper range of issues to be considered and negotiated via the forum. Many experts and scholars believe that it should be a vehicle used solely for the pursuit of trade liberalisation; others argue that it should also serve as a mechanism for the discussion of and convergence toward agreement on a range of other issues, from labour rights to environmental protections, from industrial policy to property rights.

Many experts in the last camp argue that the WTO must incorporate these broader issues into its discussions if it is to receive needed public support and secure the credibility that is required to keep trade liberalisation on track into the future. Indeed, the criticism of the WTO by the broader public is embedded in the view that the organisation has failed to account for very important 'trade-related' issues, and that it has caused considerable harm in conditions along these other dimensions. Outside of the academy and think tanks, the public criticism is immense and often withering – one need only look at the street protests in Seattle, Washington, Geneva and elsewhere for evidence of this.

These criticisms come from groups such as organised labour in the United States. The American Federation of Labor–Congress of Industrial Organisations (AFL–CIO) says on its website that:

> problems with the WTO arise because its rules favor corporate rights over social and environmental goals, and limit governments' ability to pursue those goals. Domestic laws designed to protect the environment and public health have been challenged as illegal barriers to trade by governments. In addition, under WTO rules, countries may not withdraw trade preferences from WTO members even for egregious violation of workers' rights. This has enabled large corporations to violate workers' rights, drag down living standards for workers and still enjoy free market access under WTO trade rules.[2]

These kinds of 'race-to-the-bottom' fears permeate the criticism of the WTO regarding its impact on environmental, labour, and broader regulatory policies and conditions. Many of these critics argue that the problems are so deeply established that the WTO should be abolished outright – no reform of the institution will be enough. A recent newsletter of the Sierra Club, for example, advocates this position, claiming that the WTO undermines democracy, restricts the ability of governments to pursue better public policy, and helps destroy the environment, amongst a litany of other wrongdoings.[3] Few academics, however, would argue for the elimination of the WTO, viewing its work as essential to the global economy's health.[4] But many experts believe that reforms of the WTO are needed. The Bretton Woods Committee held a forum in 2003, and the consensus was that the WTO is here to stay, though certain changes in its functions would enhance its work. The next sections of this chapter explore some of the official and non-official proposals in this area; the chapter concludes with an assessment of the competing views and my own thoughts about what should be done.

OFFICIAL VIEWS

As noted, the Meltzer Commission's focus was on possible reforms of the IMF and World Bank, rather than of the World Trade Organisation. It did, however, offer three broad recommendations for any changes in the functions of the WTO. These included:

(1)   'Rulings or decisions by the WTO, or any other multilateral entity, that extend the scope of explicit commitments under treaties or international agreements must remain subject to explicit legislative enactment by the U.S. Congress and, elsewhere, by the national legislative authority. There should be no "direct effect" on U.S. (or other) law or the ability to impose fines or penalties until national legislative ratification is completed.' (p. 108)
(2)   'The Commission proposes that, instead of retaliation, countries guilty of illegal trade practices should pay an annual fine equal to the value of the damages assessed by the panel or provide equivalent trade liberalisation.' (p. 108)
(3)   'The WTO should not extend its procedures to set domestic policies and regulations, including regulation of banking services, accounting practices, or financial standards. These should remain the responsibility of specialised agencies.' (p. 109)

The first and third of these proposed operating rules for the WTO would effectively limit the WTO's authority. While this could erode the effectiveness of the international trade rules framework, the Commission majority believes that this is needed to help promote democratic accountability and the role played by national legislatures. It also believes that the WTO should leave issues of financial stability to the World Bank and the IMF and – presumably – other issues to the appropriate, specialised organisations which might deal with them already. The second rule is grounded in the view that retaliatory tariffs are contrary to the very spirit and purpose of the WTO and generate additional harm to importing nations that use them; this mechanism also, in the Commission's view, encourages special interests to seek trade protection broadly, which hampers future efforts at trade liberalisation as well.

The US Treasury response to these Meltzer recommendations was that the use of fines rather than retaliatory tariffs in cases of treaty violations is simply not enforceable and is thus impractical – agreeing on the amount of compensation in each case is tricky, and no means exists to guarantee payment. Thus, we are left with the imperfect but workable retaliatory tariff as the sole tool for cases of transgressions. In response to the first of the Committee's proposed principles, the US Treasury (2000, p. 43) writes that it is:

based on a misunderstanding of the WTO. The United States maintains its national
sovereignty as a member of the WTO. No ruling or decision by the WTO can extend
the scope of the U.S. commitments in the WTO without explicit legislative action
by the U.S. Congress. Neither the WTO nor its dispute settlement panels can force
the United States to change its laws; only Congress can change U.S. law.[5]

In response to the dissenting view of Commissioner Levinson – who
recommends that the WTO agreement be amended to include a provision on
core workers' rights and a new chapter safeguarding more expansive
interpretations of Article XX[6] – the Treasury argues that current American
efforts at promoting stronger labour laws and conditions in other nations are
the right approach. Further, it states that the US government does not support
a new chapter nor an amendment to the charter of the WTO; rather, the
Treasury believes that consensus must be reached within the institution
about the relationship between trade and labour issues. It argues that this
should be promoted through 'active collaboration' between the WTO and the
International Labour Organisation, noting that the Clinton Administration
advocated the creation of a WTO working group on labour and trade to move
toward this end (p. 45).

As in the case of the World Bank and the IMF, the United States has pushed
for increased transparency in the operations of the WTO as an important
element in enhancing its credibility and hence its efficacy. For example, the
office of the United States Trade Representative (USTR) has encouraged the
WTO to use its website to disseminate more information and a range of
documents that are currently unavailable to the general public. In particular,
the USTR recommends that the minutes of all formal council meetings should
be made public in a much more timely fashion; the so-called Secretariat
background notes should be derestricted (made available to the public); and
the reports of all dispute settlement panels should be made public more
quickly as well. The USTR (2001) has also pushed the WTO to open its Trade
Policy Review meetings to public observation. In writing about the dispute
resolution process, it argues that:

> Increased transparency of the dispute settlement process is critical to the future of
> the WTO. If WTO dispute settlement proceedings are to play the role of ultimate
> guarantor of the system, they must be open to observation by the public, and open
> to receiving input from the public. Openness of this sort is essential to ensuring
> public support for the legitimacy of WTO dispute settlement. As the WTO takes on
> more complex and controversial cases, there is an ever-increasing need for such
> transparency. (p. 57)

In a 2001 speech to the Council on Foreign Relations, US Trade
Representative Robert Zoellick clearly articulated the position that the WTO
must tread carefully in dealing with environmental or other issues, as these can

be tied to national sovereignty.[7] No bold changes or new initiatives along these dimensions should be pushed quickly in his view.

NON-OFFICIAL VIEWS

The Bretton Woods Committee's 2003 forum brought together leading scholars and officials from around the world. Some argued that institutional reform of the WTO is not, in fact, something that should be pursued at this time; William Reinsch – President of the National Foreign Trade Council – writes that:

> Focusing on institutional reform as an alternative to trying to restart the negotiations is an attractive road to go down politically. It allows governments to postpone if not ignore the real trade issues that divide them, and it allows them to place blame on the organisation itself or, at worst, their predecessors who created it, rather than on themselves. Tempting though that is, however, I believe it is ultimately self-defeating. Its major consequence will be to postpone the day of reckoning when difficult trade issues will have to be dealt with. (Bretton Woods Committee, 2003, p. 4)

In Reinsch's opinion, the nature of the WTO as a consensus-based organisation precludes any real reform since, simply put, there is no consensus on the shape that reform should take. Further, the breakdown of negotiations is *not* prima facie evidence that the WTO needs to be reformed; history shows us that stalled talks and failed efforts are not a sign that an agreement will not be reached at some point.[8] All efforts – at least for now – should be focused on finishing the latest round of WTO talks. Most of the participants in the Bretton Woods forum, however, agreed that the WTO can do better, though they offered widely divergent views on what set of reforms should be pursued toward that end.[9] Broadly, however, many of these experts believe that any reforms would involve at least some change in the structure of governance.

Jeffrey Schott (2003) says that the WTO reform debate centres on four main issues, which include the consensus rule, the single undertaking requirement, the Dispute Settlement Understanding (DSU), and the roles of both the Secretariat and Director General of the WTO. He argues that the consensus approach is generally the right one, but that the increase in numbers of members over time has increasingly made the process unmanageable; he recommends that a new group or management committee should be formed in order to enhance the efficiency of the negotiating process. An important component of this is a more inclusive and representative membership – he notes in his earlier policy brief (Schott, 2000) that this could take the form of a reconstituted so-called Green Room consisting of twenty seats that are filled from country groupings in a way that would provide representation to nations and regions which currently have no role in its discussions.[10] He advocates that the WTO continue its single-undertaking approach to agreements, in which each nation must sign up to the entire agreement rather than select, à la carte, which requirements to meet; however, mechanisms that assist developing nations in meeting new obligations and dealing with complaints from the developed nations should also be instituted.

With regard to the DSU, Schott (2000) argued that the dispute settlement process should be allowed to take place over a longer time period, with each panel allowed to make stronger recommendations about the means by which a nation found to be in violation of negotiated outcomes will redress the problem. He also believes that panel members should be composed of experts from outside the delegates to the WTO in Geneva, in order to promote greater independence on the part of DSU panels. Finally, findings of the panels should be posted on the WTO website in a more timely fashion, in order to enhance transparency.

Schott (2003) also advocates enhanced powers on the part of the Director General, and for significant increases in the WTO budget. The Director General should, he thinks, chair WTO ministerial meetings, rather than relying on host ministers to conduct them. Forceful leadership in this form could help avoid another Seattle-style disintegration in future talks.

T.N. Srinivasan (2003) makes a bolder proposal: the membership of the WTO should elect a 'powerful executive board' as a replacement for the current consensus approach. As he notes, a single nation can effectively veto an agreement by the remaining membership, and this outcome will be more likely as the membership roster continues to expand. He also argues that it would be unwise to introduce official representation to the governance structure by adding representatives from civil society, or to allow the submission of amicus briefs to the Appellate Body of the dispute settlement mechanism. In his view, the effective operation of the WTO resides in its nature as an intergovernmental organisation – all concerns and views of broader civil societies are important and should be heard, but in the context of the national-level political processes that are channelled, as now, through the trade ministers.

This point is echoed in Rugman (2001), in a discussion of the international political environment in recent years, and the effect of changes there on the performance of the WTO. He writes, in reference to the prominence afforded non-governmental organisations (NGOs) at the Seattle Round of talks, that:

> the WTO may fail because its acute lack of political skill led it to make the dreadful mistake of giving standing to non-governmental organisations at the abortive Seattle Millennium Rounds of December 1999. For the WTO to succeed it must only work with governments, as it was designed to do. This is what the GATT did. The

members of the GATT/WTO are nations, not firms, not NGOs. Each government negotiates on behalf of its businesses and NGOs. (p. 19)

He concludes that multilateralism is being eroded by the presence of NGOs at the WTO forums, and that it is imperative that they be excluded from participation in future rounds of talks. The same, of course, applies to business groups and interests.

Paula Stern (2003, p. 10), former chairperson of the US International Trade Commission, also makes the case that a change in the governance structure of the WTO is needed, writing that:

the WTO governance structure must be revamped to de-politicise the Secretariat's day-to-day work. The top-level Ministerial conference should continue meeting at regular, but infrequent intervals. However, the second-tier General Council should be rebuilt on the model of the IMF Executive Board, where large trading powers maintain individual representation, and smaller commercial powers organise into blocs.

She notes that a Latin America bloc, for example, could select as a representative a member of a negotiating team that has produced a regional trade agreement in the past, or perhaps an accomplished diplomat from a Latin American nation.

Others are not optimistic that any real reforms of the governance structure of the WTO are likely. Odell (2001, p. 26) believes that the possibilities described above are not to be practicably achieved. He writes that instead:

it is much more likely that members will keep the structure weak at the centre and the transaction costs of consensus high. Thus, with a much larger active membership, stalemates will be more difficult to overcome and will last longer. Individual members get limited help from the centre in devising and implementing integrative strategies.

He concludes that the most plausible scenario is continued stalemate at the WTO, with trade liberalisation taking place through regional and bilateral agreements instead, with the energy and focus of leading developed nations dedicated to other tasks and goals. These efforts might include enlargement of the European Union, or a deepening of current agreements like the NAFTA into, say, a Free Trade Area of the Americas.

As with the official views discussed above, much of the attention of other experts and scholars has focused on the possibility of linking trade talks with other issues and agendas, from environmental policies to labour standards and more, within the WTO framework itself. This is in response to the many public pressures placed on the WTO to move in that direction. This discussion is at a very early stage, though some important themes are emerging. Needless to say, there is a deep disagreement about so-called 'trade linkages'. Many scholars argue that the job of the WTO is daunting enough, and all energies should be devoted to eliminating any remaining obstacles to free trade, to resolving deadlock on agricultural subsidies, and so on. Other experts claim that not only does the WTO not have the political ability to ignore these other issues, but that it makes economic sense for it to take them into account. This debate is intense, and the arguments at times complex. As Jackson (2002, p. 118) writes:

> The problem of linkages between 'non-trade' subjects and the World Trade organisation is certainly one of the most pressing and challenging policy puzzles for international economic relations and institutions today. It is extensively and harshly debated by political leaders and diplomats, at both the national and international levels of discourse, and is one of several issues that derailed the WTO Third Ministerial Conference in Seattle in late 1999.

As Jackson notes, the problem has not receded since then and could, he believes, threaten to derail the WTO as an institution. We suspect that most experts would agree with this assessment.

Several other experts have noted that this issue is not a new one: it has been with us since the founding of the GATT over fifty years ago. Debra Steger (2002, p. 135), former Director of the Appellate Body Secretariat of the WTO, writes that:

> The issue of whether and how the trading system should deal with the social and economic policies not strictly within the ambit of the WTO has been with us since the inception of the GATT in 1947–48. It is not a new question. The problem, however, has become more vexing since the 1970s, as tariffs became less important in trading relationships and governments struggled to respond to the proliferation of non-tariff barriers to trade … the question is not whether the WTO should or should not deal with 'trade and …' subjects – trade and environment, trade and public health, trade and labour rights, trade and human rights, trade and competition, trade and investment, and trade and intellectual property, to name a few. It already does and has done so, in many respects, since 1948.

In Steger's estimation, the real debate is thus about exactly *how* (rather than whether) these non-trade subjects ought to be handled by the WTO – it also is about who should define the exact scope of the WTO involvement in these. Should that be determined by all the members of the organisation, or rather by the dispute resolution panels or perhaps the Appellate Body? We now turn our attention to this debate, beginning with a discussion of the arguments offered in favour of a broader mandate for the WTO.

Richardson (2001) argues that the WTO is indeed the proper forum for a discussion of, and negotiations over, what he labels 'market-supportive regulations'. In his view, the WTO has already incorporated some of these into its past work – these would include its recent efforts regarding Trade-Related Aspects of Intellectual Property Rights (TRIPS) as well as telecommunications. He makes the broad case that market-supportive competition policies are within the broad rubric of WTO work since they and multilateral trade negotiations both share the same overarching goal: to create 'more open, contestable, non-discriminatory market organisation of economic activity' (p. 260). Thus, it is natural that the WTO undertake multilateral negotiations over competition conditions and policies broadly, albeit at a slow pace.

Among the initial set of competition policies that he advocates the WTO discuss is modification to the current TRIPS Agreement. In his view, that agreement has been an important component in fostering the production of intellectual property, but it has failed to facilitate the orderly distribution of that property. That is, the agreement has not helped create the appropriate conditions for the 'retail market' in intellectual property. He offers two modifications of the TRIPS framework. The first would be the creation of a fee imposed on cross-border royalties generated on intellectual property; these funds could then be used to provide loans to countries that are tightening IP protections, but which need financial support to develop the necessary institutions. The actual programme would be run by others (he suggests local patent offices or public–private consortia). He also believes that a consensus on arranging a standstill on TRIPS requirements would be helpful; allowing each nation to develop its own set of standards and competition policies would itself foster innovation in the mechanisms that help provide IP protection. Thus, instead of using the WTO to pursue deeper TRIPS-style agreements and conditions, attention should first be devoted to developing such a standstill period.

He likewise argues – more provocatively – that the WTO is also the right place for the pursuit of an agreement on at least some labour market regulations, arguing that many of these can be viewed as attempts to liberalise what he labels 'worker–agency services'. The WTO – which has already worked towards liberalising services generally – is thus the right place to 'park' these efforts. He cites freedom of association and collective bargaining as the specific agenda to begin WTO efforts in this area. He writes that open trade in worker–agency services is:

> entirely conformable to the WTO's endorsement of open trade in other services. We understand such worker–agency services to encompass primarily collective representation and bargaining over wages, benefits, and working conditions; workplace safety monitoring; grievance and dispute settlement; training, apprenticeship, and employee assistance, financial counsel (for example, pensions) and management of other benefits (for example, child care). (Richardson, 2001, p. 265)

Richardson notes that these services are market-supportive in that they help resolve market failures that arise from collective action problems, lack of workplace public goods, and imperfect information. The efficiency of providing these will be enhanced if not only local but global suppliers are able to offer them to workers within any nation. In this respect, trade in these worker–agency services is much the same as trade in accounting, legal, and brokerage services, to name but a few.

Richardson acknowledges, however, that this will be viewed as a radical idea. Thus, it is important to proceed 'modestly and procedurally' (p. 266). He suggests that a Trade-Related Worker Agency Services (TWAS) Agreement should only be pursued after unilateral efforts have been undertaken – that is, nations could individually implement labour standards and policies, without a broader formal dispute mechanism yet available. Further, such a TWAS Agreement should focus only on freedom of association and collective bargaining, and perhaps only in certain key sectors or industries of the economy. At later stages, it could be deepened and broadened.

Bagwell et al. (2002) explore the theoretical underpinnings behind the linking of traditional trade liberalisation efforts and other reforms (like those espoused by Richardson). Their basic argument is that:

> market access issues associated with the question of the optimal mandate of the World Trade Organisation should be separated from non-market access issues. We identify race-to-the-bottom and regulatory-chill concerns as market access issues and suggest that the WTO should address these concerns ... as for non-market access issues, we argue that as a general matter these are best handled outside the WTO, and that, while implicit links might be encouraged, explicit links between the WTO and other labour and environmental organisations should not as a general matter be forged. (p. 56)

Noting that the WTO is a forum for governments to negotiate over market access and to avoid the prisoners' dilemma inherent in unilateral, non-cooperative decision-making, the authors point out that the WTO, and the GATT before it, have recognised that meaningful market access cannot be secured with trade liberalisation alone. Many governments seek to secure access to other nations' markets (and thus experience a positive terms-of-trade effect) through a promise to provide access as well in the form of lower trade barriers, yet in turn effectively bar such access through policy changes in areas outside of trade policy. They note that WTO rules that proscribe discriminatory treatment of foreign products generally are intended to cement meaningful market access through trade liberalisation. Thus, 'we may interpret GATT articles as (1) facilitating negotiations that lead to mutually advantageous increases in market access levels, and (2) creating a system of property rights over negotiated market access commitments that are secure against unilateral governmental infringement' (p. 59).

In their formulation, a nation that unilaterally lowers, say, its environmental standards for its import-competing industries in order to give them a leg-up (through lower production costs) vis-à-vis their foreign competitors will fail to help deliver a globally optimal level of market access because it fails to internalise the cost of reduced market access for its trade partners. As Bagwell et al. (2000, p. 56) say, 'this fundamental problem is then manifested through the unilateral determination of the various policy instruments, with import tariffs that are too high and/or standards in import-competing industries that are too low'.

In this plan a commitment by one government to another to provide greater market access can be achieved through a variety of standards-cum-trade barrier combinations. Thus, there is a menu or 'mix' (to use these authors' term) of such combinations from which a nation is able to deliver a given level of market access to other nations. Whether a government chooses a high standards–high tariff mix or a low tariff–low standards mix in its import-competing sectors is not important *if* the only concern is the degree of market access provided to its trading partners (through its total array of trade and standards policies). Put in their words, 'government A's polices are relevant in government B's view only insofar as they affect the terms of trade and thus the overall access of country B's exporters to country A's market' (p. 61).

Using this analytical framework, Bagwell et al. explore several issues in the current debate over globalisation, including race-to-the-bottom concerns, 'regulatory chill,' and – of course – the scope of trade and standards linkages to be incorporated into the WTO forum. They conclude that the current policy options that are available to governments under WTO obligations could, in fact, encourage, at least in theory, a race-to-the-bottom in terms of environmental, labour and other standards. As they note:

> under GATT/WTO rules a government cannot respond to competitive pressures abroad by unilaterally restricting market access with an increase in its tariff (unless it is willing to pay compensation), the government may be tempted to restrict access by reducing standards in its import-competing industry. Second, if a government increases standards in its import-competing industry, this industry would be subjected to increased competitive pressure from abroad, but the government would not be allowed under GATT/WTO rules to raise its tariff (without compensation) and maintain its market access commitment. Consequently, the government might refrain from raising standards in an import-competing industry, since some of its benefits would flow to foreign exporters. (p. 61)

They describe these GATT/WTO rules as 'imperfections in property rights over market access commitments' which impinge upon governments' abilities to deal with increased foreign competition. These can encourage governments to lower standards (the race-to-the-bottom phenomena) or resist raising them (the regulatory chill phenomena) – these imperfections are the genuine source of these trends, rather than lower standards in developing nations per se.

Thus, the WTO can serve as the appropriate venue for the development and promulgation of labour, environmental, or other standards that affect market access across borders; the authors suggest that the Articles of Agreement could be amended or interpreted to allow for, when needed, compensation to exporters in exchange for an increase in a nation's tariff along with higher standards in any of these areas. Further, the Articles could be modified to discourage regulatory chill by adding language that suggests that WTO members who raise these standards can also raise import tariffs without any additional compensation to exporting nations, if so desired. This change would also, of course, include mechanisms for dispute resolution in case of disagreement about the permissibility of any mix of policy changes.

Extending their analysis, the authors examine when – if ever – the WTO should serve as the appropriate forum for dealing with non-pecuniary externalities; these are actions or policies of governments that do not (only) affect market competitiveness but the more general well-being of other nations more broadly. The classic example, of course, would be lax environmental standards in one nation which allow its firms to generate pollution that spills over the border and affects the environment of other countries. A more provocative illustration provided by these authors has to do with labour law. They write that:

> country A's weak labour standards may provoke 'humanitarian' concerns in country B, if the government of country B has a direct concern for the well-being of workers in country A. And second, weak labour standards and poor social conditions in country A may contribute, in the words of the preamble of the ILO Constitution, to social 'unrest so great that the peace and harmony of the world are imperilled,' and thus give rise to political concerns in country B. (p. 69)

The solution is to incorporate negotiations over labour, environmental, and other standards which affect market access into the WTO framework as a means of creating greater flexibility in determining the division of benefits from cooperative agreements on all fronts – Bagwell et al. note that in the 1980s many nations entered into debt-for-environment swaps, and that many developed nations impose certain requirements on the local standards adopted by developing countries that must be met in order to receive financial assistance. This suggests, of course, that such linkages between trade liberalisation and other policies or standards might best be made outside of the WTO (perhaps, for example, as part of bilateral trade agreements or for access to GSP – generalised system of preferences – lists). But, in many cases, the WTO could be the appropriate vehicle for the establishment of such linkages.

Many others are sceptical of the appropriateness of linking trade liberalisation and other issues, whether generally or under the auspices of the GATT/WTO. Ederington (2002) uses a game theoretic model to explore the conditions under which such linkages are indeed optimal, given possible mechanisms through which enforcement is provided. He concludes that only when an international agreement is enforced by the threat of autarkic sanctions is policy linkage of any benefit – in his model, without that severe form of sanction for violations of existing agreements, nations will typically be tempted to deviate from their obligations under domestic standards provisions. He then notes that the threat of autarky is not plausible since its very severity makes it not credible as a policy option. Thus, 'the benefits of "policy linkage" may be lower than is commonly thought, since policy linkage is only beneficial in those agreements that are supported by the implicit threat of autarky trade sanctions' (p. 1364).

Leebron (2002) provides a survey of the issues involved in linkages in international negotiations broadly, both in terms of the reasons why these might be pursued and the mechanisms by which they can be established. He notes that a distinction needs to be made between what he labels 'strategic linkages' (those that are made simply as a device to strategically obtain desired outcomes in an area) versus 'non-strategic linkages' (those that promote greater efficiency or optimality generally). He concludes that:

> Linking highly divisive issues on which there is no point of agreement between the two parties can potentially inhibit agreement on the entire group of linked issues, including those on which agreement would have been possible in the absence of the linked issues. In general, the greater the number of linked issues, and the more controversial those issues, the less likely it will be for an agreement to be reached. When, however, issues are controversial in the sense that most outcomes will have highly skewed distributional consequences, it may ease negotiations to link the issues to another controversial issue ... thus, one cannot argue as a general matter that strategic considerations militate for or against linkage; it will depend on the circumstances. (p. 25)

He notes that the GATT/WTO have already begun to establish linkages between trade liberalisation and other issues, writing that 'they have moved from a wooden, formalistic approach that largely ignored the evolution of international environmental law, to one that tries in a nuanced way to incorporate this evolution into a dynamic interpretation of the GATT rules' (p. 27). He thinks, however, that – in general – the use of one regime (such as the WTO) to advance the interests of another area is sub-optimal; it is better to develop the regime (the organisation and sets of agreements) that specialises in those other areas.

Charnovitz (2002) provides another analytical framework for assessing the proper scope of WTO issues; he notes that the answer to this requires a deeper, more complete understanding of the purposes and the objectives of the organisation. He believes that, in fact, the mission of the WTO is not all that obvious. He proposes the use of eight 'frames' that help assess the implications of state-to-state relations, domestic politics, and international organisational architecture for the scope of WTO functions. He believes that collectively these lead us to believe that the WTO should focus its efforts on those areas in which cooperative behaviour across nations is problematic and needs support. Further, those efforts should include those that help achieve convergence of national policies, regulations, and standards; promote the equitable treatment of nations by other nations; promulgate rules that reduce arbitrary and unpredictable governmental actions (that is, help mitigate risks for private economic actors); serve as a forum for helping curb domestic protectionist sentiments and pressures within nations;[11] help national leaders work toward establishing coalitions within their borders that support trade liberalisation or other efforts of the WTO; allow the WTO either to expand or narrow its scope at the behest of member organisations who can – as they have already – amend the Articles of Agreement as desired; and carefully survey the roles played by and the efficacy of other international organisations in order to determine if the WTO is the best place to situate any particular issue.

Charnovitz does not intend his analysis to supply us with a definitive, particular answer about the proper scope and mission of the WTO, but rather to provide a clearer set of guiding principles to be used to move us toward that answer. However, he does offer several suggestive illustrations about how these eight principles may be defined and applied. He argues, for example, that with reference to the role of helping curb domestic political pressures that:

> If the WTO's purpose is to assist governments in overcoming rent-seeking interests at home, then other policies involving vested interests from governmental regulation might be candidates for WTO oversight. One example would be the allocation of portions of the electromagnetic spectrum. At present, the only relevant WTO discipline is contained in the reference paper for basic telecommunications, which commits participating governments to allocating electromagnetic frequency bands 'in an objective, timely, transparent and non-discriminatory fashion.' Another example would be the allocation of airport landing rights. (p. 45)

An expanded scope for the organisation suggested by this risk-reduction frame might be the establishment of basic WTO rules regarding the treatment of direct foreign or portfolio investment; he quotes the former European Commissioner for Trade, Pascal Lamy, who said that 'increasing the predictability for potential investors would lead to more investment with all the benefits that it can bring'.[12] He also argues broadly, as another example, that core labour standards are appropriate to the scope of the WTO mission via the role in fostering convergence in standards and policies across countries.

Charnovitz acknowledges that expansion of WTO duties and mission must be undertaken cautiously rather than aggressively. Using the principle that the WTO must survey the roles of other institutions, he writes that:

> Sometimes the WTO cannot be directly compared to an alternative IGO because there is none. In that situation, resort to the WTO should be compared to the option of leaving needed government cooperation to bilateral agreements or informal arrangements. Because its rules are backed by a strong enforcement system, the WTO should be careful about articulating new disciplines on topics facing an international organisation that might serve as a check against WTO overreaching. (p. 53)

Here he cites the example of the property rights of indigenous peoples over traditional knowledge – no institution or framework is yet in place to deal with this issue, and he suggests that the TRIPS Agreement could actually have adverse consequences for these groups.

Bhagwati (2002) makes the argument that the Bretton Woods institutions – including the GATT/WTO – should be 'geared to providing compensation or adjustment assistance to poor countries harmed by the freeing of trade' (p. 127). By this measure, he believes that the TRIPS Agreement is inappropriate as it extracts, in effect, royalty payments from poorer developing nations to developed nations who produce intellectual property. With this in mind he argues that:

> We ... demonstrated to the next set of northern lobbies that they could do the same. Thus, the unions now say: you did it for 'capital' so do it for 'labour'; and the environmental lobbies say: you did it for capital, so do it for 'nature'. And the poor countries that have no lobbies anywhere like the sumptuous ones such as the Sierra Club and the AFL–CIO now find themselves at the receiving end of a growing list of lobbying demands that the northern politicians are ready to concede, cynically realising that a bone thrown to those lobbies in their own political spaces is a bone down the gullets of the poor nations. (p. 128)

He argues that the TRIPS Agreement is one leg of the WTO that should *not* be in place, and that the addition of other issues will effectively turn the forum into a 'centipede' with more and more appendages, which he believes would seriously impede meaningful trade liberalisation and in turn do serious harm to less-developed nations. He is not convinced that related issues can be brought into the WTO framework as an element of market access discussions, partly because this would open the door to just about everything under the sun. He notes that 'we must really pause before we drag into WTO jurisprudence and practice others' differences in domestic policies and institutions claiming in effect that any such differences are to be the stuff of which "unfair trade" charges of denial of negotiated market access are made' (p. 129). He proposes that the only appropriate linkages to be made are to those very proximate standards and practices that can be construed to pertain to 'competition policy' in the narrow, traditional sense of the word.

Bhagwati goes on to explore in particular the possibility of linking trade liberalisation talks under the WTO to certain labour issues (such as those raised by Bagwell and Staiger, 1999, and Richardson, 2001). He argues that on neither narrowly self-interested nor altruistic grounds can a real case be made for the *need* to link labour standards to trade talks. He suggests that there is no empirical support for the claim of race-to-the-bottom phenomena, nor real evidence that liberalised trade – even with developing nations – has contributed to any significant degree to the stagnation or decline of real wages of certain groups in advanced nations. In the same way, he points to research that supports the view that trade liberalisation has improved average living standards and has helped reduce the incidence of poverty in the less-developed parts of the world. Trade sanctions or other efforts to broadly impose conditions on labour market policy as part of trade agreements has – he says – had perverse results: stop importing textiles from Southeast Asia because of their labour standards and you will find more women and children engaged in prostitution and the drug trade. He further argues that the issues we want to grapple with are simply too complex to fall under the purview of the GATT/WTO, writing that:

> I would stress that the WTO does not begin to qualify to be the institution to manage the complex issues raised by 'core labour standards' concepts such as the right to unionise and the absence of gender discrimination. Take just the latter. Even if we were to take merely the question of equal pay within its vast scope, such equality can be defined in different ways. Is it just payment of identical wages for equal merit when both men and women work for the American Society of International Law? Or is it also equal pay across different sectors for equal qualifications as determined, for instance by a pay commission in several countries? Or do we raise questions of metapreferences and ask why women gravitate toward lower-paying occupations and what we need to do about it in terms of gender identity formation, values formation, role-playing and so forth. Does anyone expect that all this can be sorted out at the WTO? (Bhagwati, 2002, p. 132)

Bhagwati is also opposed to the use of trade policy on the basis of moral concerns or issues; allowing nations to prohibit the importation of products that they view as being produced in unethical ways will open a Pandora's box, and set us on a slippery slope toward reduced global trade.

Jackson (2002) likewise discusses the possibility of trade linkages to other issues being put under the purview of the GATT/WTO. He argues that the view that the institution should return to a 'core mission' of solely focusing on multilateral attempts to reduce border measures is a seriously flawed one: the very history of these institutions has reflected an attempt to ascertain that internal national policies more broadly do not mitigate the trade liberalisation that has been negotiated through GATT/WTO agreements. He cites the 'national treatment' clause of Article III of the GATT as one example of a norm that seeks to ensure that nations do not adopt discriminatory practices which effectively curb imports from other GATT members. What remains, he notes, is the appropriate boundary for trade–other issue linkages.

His approach in determining this is to consider the relevance of sovereignty, subsidiarity, and process: should the norms and rules be hammered out via negotiations by all parties, or by an institution charged with their development? Should this process take place at the global level, or across more local (or national) jurisdictions? The answers, he believes, are ultimately grounded in an empirical analysis of the capabilities and characteristics of current institutions; the effectiveness and the soundness of these must be assessed in order to determine what more or less they ought to be doing. He considers the possibility of putting antitrust or anti-cartel regulations within the WTO forum by asking four questions: is there a need for governmental action, particularly as implied by globalisation? If so, is international coordination really needed or can individual nation-states better handle these? If the former, does an existing framework exist to deal with the policies? If not, does a cost–benefit analysis suggest that either new frameworks must be instituted, or that existing ones need to be modified in order to accommodate them?

Jackson does not supply an answer to these questions; he rather makes the point that to provide one requires a rich, deep empirical understanding of global conditions, institutions, and characteristics. This implies, he thinks, that the answer to the linkages issue that is at the forefront of the current debate about the WTO must come from what he labels a 'bottom-up' approach: specific cases or possible issues linkages must be thought through on a case-by-case basis, rather than via a single broad principle of how linkages are to be made, if at all. He thus cautions against a general formula or definitive statement about the inclusion of linked issues in the GATT/WTO forums.

Rodrik (2001) proposes that any reform of the international institutions must be guided by four basic principles (my labels, not his): democratic discipline, national rootedness, institutional diversity, and prosperity maximisation. His first tenet – democratic discipline – says that public policy is best tempered, monitored, and influenced not by market forces but rather by democratic processes; he believes that 'civil liberties, political freedom, and participatory procedures are the best way to ensure appropriate labour standards, environmental sustainability, and economic stability' (p. 1). Market-based disciplines are, he argues, too volatile, narrowly focused (on financial considerations), and short-sighted to serve that purpose. His second guiding principle is that the locus of democratic participation must still be the nation-state, rather than a transnational institution or groups that operate globally – he is sceptical of the ability of international NGOs, for example, to function in a truly democratic fashion. Further, his third and fourth tenets are that democratic institutions must and should be diverse in form across the globe, taking into account local cultures and norms, and that the objectives of the WTO (and World Bank or IMF) should not be to maximise economic integration but rather to maximise 'thickness' in economic transactions in a way consistent with maintaining diversity in national institutions. He argues that 'instead of asking "how can we maximise the flow of goods and capital around the world?" we would ask "how can we ensure that all countries simultaneously prosper within their own social arrangements?" This would entail a significant shift in the mindset of negotiators in the national arena' (p. 2).

He notes that an implication of this would be that international economic rules and agreements must build in more 'opt-out' or exit clauses when the obligations entailed by these agreements conflict with nations' other priorities. To prevent this from devolving into simple unilateralism, he argues that the procedural requirements and safeguards must be negotiated ex ante – since this mechanism is needed to attain compatibility between economic integration and national democratic institutions, authoritarian regimes would not be entitled to the same opt-out privilege. He ends by writing that:

> Markets require governance. Good governance can be ensured only via democracy. And democracy remains co-extensive with the nation state. These simple facts impose serious limits on how far we can push global economic integration and international institutionalisation. Ignoring this is a recipe for economic failure and social instability. (p. 3)

Rodrik (2002) makes similar points, but offers an even more striking observation: 'the political trilemma of the global economy is that the nation-state system, democratic politics, and full economic integration are mutually incompatible' (p. 1). He argues that markets function effectively only when they are embedded in well-established non-market institutions, which help regulate, confer legitimacy on, and stabilise markets themselves; further, there is no unique correspondence between these institutional roles and the particular form that these institutions must take. In fact, this variety of national institutions is necessary for the promotion of economic development across a range of cultures and social realities.

However, this sort of natural institutional diversity is in turn an impediment to complete economic integration. He cites the ongoing presence of non-trade barriers – in the form of what he labels heterogeneous national institutions – as evidence of this.

Given the inherent tension between the existence of nation-states, institutional diversity, and complete economic integration, the question then becomes one of which of these must give in to or yield to the other two (any pair is, in Rodrik's estimation, compatible). Given that the prospects for a true global government or state are rather dim, and that very few would agree to forgo democratic governance, he concludes that we must abandon our attempts to establish *complete* economic integration. He also argues that we need to establish much clearer rules for this less ambitious kind of global economic integration. He notes that the reality of the original Bretton Woods–GATT system was that countries were allowed to maintain certain kinds of barriers to full economic integration – such as restrictions on financial capital flows – as long as they agreed to eliminate trade restrictions in a non-discriminatory fashion. The push toward much more comprehensive economic integration only began in the 1980s and into the last decade. We must, he argues, return to some version of the earlier Bretton Woods approach.

While Rodrik does not offer a complete menu of reforms to the international organisations, he discusses the issue of labour mobility to illustrate his point and to provide a possible starting point for the kinds of broader reforms he advocates. He maintains that if the goal of international trade talks is to boost global income – especially in the Third World – the proper strategy is the design of policies that promote international labour flows, rather than the elimination of more trade barriers, reduction of agricultural subsidies, or the promotion of protection of intellectual property rights. The latter will generate fairly small income gains for developing nations; a much bigger bang can be gotten from a relaxation of restrictions on labour mobility across borders (especially of course, between developed and less-developed nations). By his (back-of-the-envelope) estimate this would generate up to twenty-five times higher benefits than would the more traditional reforms promoted by the WTO. He proposes that advanced economies could, for example, introduce a temporary work visa scheme that would allow up to the equivalent of 3 per cent of the domestic labour force – for a period of three to five years – a temporary foreign work force with a skill composition approximately equal to the local labour force to enter developed nations. Upon returning to their home nations, these temporary workers would bring with them newly-acquired skills and the human capital that they accrued through that work experience. Of course, incentives would need to be implemented to ensure that temporary workers returned to their home nations, rather than trying to remain in developed nations at the end of their visits. One possibility that Rodrik suggests is a withholding scheme that sets aside some of the workers' wages which are released only upon departure.

Rodrik acknowledges that the political opposition to such a programme might seem insurmountable. However, he argues that this is not the case – after all, imports from developing nations into developed nations have (in theory) the same effect on relative real incomes as do labour flows. The only reason that trade liberalisation has been realisable in developed nations is because of the ability of groups that benefit from it to more readily organise and lobby than those who might be opposed to it. As he notes,

> Temporary labour flows, by contrast, have not had a well-defined constituency in the advanced countries. This is not because the benefits are smaller, but because the beneficiaries are not as clearly identifiable. When a Turkish worker enters the European Union or a Mexican worker enters the US, the ultimate beneficiaries in Europe and the US are not known ex ante. It is only after a worker lands a job that his employer has a direct stake in keeping him in the country. This explains why, for example, the US federal government spends a large amount of resources on border controls to prevent hypothetical immigrants from coming in, while it has virtually no ability to deport employed illegals or fine their employers once they are actually inside the country. (p. 22)

Thus, the public is 'trainable' on this point. Economists need only devote as much energy to explaining the benefits of relaxed labour movement restrictions as they do reduced trade barriers in order to convince the public of the merits of this kind of policy.[13]

The World Bank (2004) explores the issues around (temporary) labour movements, noting that the General Agreement on Trade in Services (GATS) of the WTO already allows for the temporary movement of certain kinds of workers across member nations. The provisions of the so-called Mode 4 of the GATS, however, generally focus on the mobility of higher-skilled workers; about 50 per cent of the commitments made in this agreement are business visitors, executives and managers, and about 40 per cent are what may be considered intra-corporate movements related to direct foreign investment (p. 144). The World Bank thus concludes that 'all this means that Mode 4 liberalisation achieved to date has been of limited significance for developing countries whose comparative advantage lies in the export of medium- and low-skilled, labour intensive services' (p. 144).

The World Bank report goes on to argue that – while the gains from deeper liberalisation of temporary labour movement on a multilateral basis might indeed be quite sizeable – progress on this front is not likely because of the political opposition to this kind of policy. They suggest that the right approach in negotiations over Mode 4 in the Doha Round is to focus on expanding the scope for worker movement according to national comparative advantages; this could imply (in my thinking) that rather than pursue a blanket, across-the-board liberalisation, member nations might focus on negotiating labour mobility rules for key sectors.

A final set of proposals worth considering come from the WTO, World Bank, and the IMF themselves. These are still rather inchoate, but seem to provide some broad parameters about the direction of internal reforms of the WTO. Over the past few years, representatives from the three organisations have met to discuss 'coherence' across their respective policies and practices. In its 2003 coherence report, the WTO notes that:

> The IMF and the World Bank can also help reassure developing and least-developed countries that they will receive technical and financial support for trade liberalisation and reform within their fragile economic environments – to correct temporary external balances; to manage any loss of fiscal revenue from reducing tariffs; to weather a period of adjusting to the erosion of trade preferences, to secure adequate and reliable trade-financing facilities; and, above all, to take advantage of increased export opportunities by investing in trade-related institutions and infrastructure and in the supply side of their economies. (WTO, 2003, p. 2)

In order to facilitate that work, the WTO secretariat proposes that each organisation should be granted observer status in the Trade Negotiating Committee; they should identify ways in which they can facilitate and speed up WTO accession procedures for low-income developing nations, especially when trade reform is a key component of economic development for these countries; the Bank and Fund should play a critical role in determining the sequence of economic reforms and in the development of adjustment assistance programmes that help achieve poverty reduction in a meaningful way.

The WTO report identifies key areas for the development of rules and procedures on the part of all three organisations: the IMF and WTO should determine the circumstances under which the Fund might ask a member to enact capital account transactions that are inconsistent with obligations under Article XI of the General Agreement on Trade in Services; the Fund and WTO ought to work on reforms to balance-of-payments safeguard provisions if international investment becomes an important component of multilateral trade talks; the Bank, Fund, and the WTO should collectively develop practices and policies around trade-financing assistance during financial crises (such as the 1997 South East Asia Crisis); they should also work toward dealing with significant devaluations that trigger complaints of 'unfair trade practices' by advanced nations; and seek to assure that policy prescriptions and conditionality requirements of all three organisations are consistent and not at cross-purposes. The latter is particularly important as this affects the development agenda each is pursuing.

The most recent report on coherence (World Trade Organisation, 2004) provides an update on efforts in these directions. The three organisations believe that their collective efforts should centre on trade liberalisation efforts – particularly in the area of agriculture – that stand to benefit less-developed nations, and as promulgated in the Doha Round of trade negotiations. They note that, while reforms and liberalisation that might be achieved through these talks stand to generate significant benefits for less-developed nations, they could also impose substantial short-term adjustment costs on these same countries. Thus, they feel that serious efforts should be made at providing financial assistance to help in this regard. Further, the IMF and the World Bank are to take the lead in providing this – this is because they, and not the WTO, are organisationally equipped at the moment to do this. Also, many IMF Board members feel that the so-called Compensatory Financing Facility (CFF) of the Fund should be eliminated given the low demand for its services and assistance.[14]

While much of the discussion in this report focuses on technical and advisory assistance to less-developed nations as they liberalise trade, a brief review of the organisations' efforts to provide more substantial financial assistance is provided. The report notes that the IMF has introduced its Trade Integration Mechanism to provide for balance-of-payment support for short-term needs induced by multilateral trade reforms. It also notes that the World Bank recently announced that it will seek to provide additional funds:

> devoted to trade logistics (e.g. transport costs) and trade facilitation, in addition to enhanced sectoral lending in support of programmes designed to protect workers and vulnerable groups, and programme lending for countries implementing development-related Doha trade reforms. This reflects a longer-term trend of World Bank instruments for supporting country-level trade activities away from adjustment lending for the purpose of supporting the liberalisation of border measures, towards the increased use of a wider array of instruments for addressing trade issues. (p. 11)

These latter efforts include capacity-building, technical, and institution-building support.

Based on our earlier discussion, I believe that the proper division of labour and the suggestion that the mission scope of all three organisations should be more focused implies that the Bank should indeed concentrate efforts on improved infrastructure (for example, port and transportation networks) that facilitates trade, among other efforts that might be viewed as functions traditional to its mission. This would, in my view, include a shift toward the priorities highlighted by the Copenhagen Consensus, as discussed in Chapter 5.

But this also suggests that the assistance provided to less-developed nations for workers who might be adversely impacted by trade reform could be moved to the World Trade Organisation itself. I suggest that the possibility of negotiating transnational transfer payments for this purpose be added to the current negotiations under the Doha Round. These transfers would be channelled to the least-advantaged workers in less-developed nations. This kind of programme would, given the nature and configuration of the organisation's current institutions, require a new Council – this would be the Council for Global Trade Adjustment Assistance.

Of critical importance would be the source of funds for this programme. Once source – albeit a controversial one – would be the earmarking of a certain, negotiated percentage of the remaining tariffs in all member states to be used for trade adjustment assistance (TAA) programmes. I propose that developed nations in turn allocate a negotiated percentage of these dedicated funds to developing nations for that purpose. As part of this, remaining quantitative restrictions would need to be converted into tariff equivalents with those collections included in this scheme. It would be up to each nation to design – with the assistance of the World Bank – a particular design of a TAA programme within its borders. Disbursement of funds could take place via the Bank or the regional development banks, keeping the WTO as a forum rather than a 'beefed-up' organisation. Of course, as tariffs are reduced through any negotiated outcome, TAA funds for the purpose of assisting with adjustments due to WTO obligations would decrease – this seems natural, as the need for them, because of reductions due to commitments themselves, should not be persistent. Of course, each nation would likely find it in its interest to find the mechanism – whether traditional unemployment programmes or general Trade Adjustment Assistance programmes – to provide the social safety net for workers displaced due to shifting comparative advantage or sudden changes in terms-of-trade. Of course, current provisions within the WTO that help nations deal with so-called import surges are one piece of this; however, broader political support for further economic integration could be more easily secured with more substantial assistance to those groups who experience decreases in employment prospects and real income because of global conditions.[15]

NOTES

1. He also examines the role of the IMF in promoting trade via its conditionality requirements.
2. Taken from the 2005 policy statement 'What is the WTO?' by the AFL–CIO (American Federation of Labor–Congress of Industrial Organisations).
3. See Mokhiber and Weissman (1999); the Sierra Club does not broadly advocate the elimination of the WTO, but stresses the need for serious reform to promote fair and just trade.
4. The bottom line is its work to promote efficiency gains through pursuit of comparative advantage, which individual nations fail to do consistently because of special interests and the domestic political process. Irwin (2000, p. 353) argues that the role of the WTO in this regard is thus primarily political: 'the WTO is useful because it changes the political economy of trade policy in a way that tends to facilitate trade liberalisation as an outcome'.
5. Many other experts make this point. See, for example, Lash (2000) and Jackson (1994).
6. Article XX addresses exceptions to negotiated outcomes. It reads: 'Subject to the requirement that such measures are not applied in a manner which would constitute a means of arbitrary or unjustifiable discrimination between countries where the same conditions prevail, or a disguised restriction on international trade, nothing in the Agreement shall be construed to prevent the adoption or enforcement by any contracting party of measures.' Some of the valid reasons for exceptions include those necessary to protect public morals;

necessary to protect human, animal or plant life or health; and those relating to the importations or exportations of gold or silver.

7. Though Zoellick (2001, p. 7) noted that 'the United States would welcome increased interaction between the WTO and the secretariats of Multilateral Environmental Agreements', and that the WTO should be invited to contribute to the work of the ILO and other organisations in promoting international core labour standards. No particular details were provided.

8. As this is written, in fact, the Doha Round has been revitalised with the movement by the US and Europe on agricultural subsidies; the optimism that this will push the talks forward is palpable.

9. They also disagreed on when reforms should be pursued. Ellen Frost and Frederick Montgomery make the case that reform is best pursued in a 'climate of success' (Bretton Woods Committee, 2003, p. 2). They believe that reforms must await the successful conclusion of the Doha Round, and a less politically-charged atmosphere in the United States.

10. The so-called Green Room of the WTO is the informal discussions between leading nations – including the USA, European countries, Japan, and so on – that precede and shape formal talks.

11. This brings to mind Irwin's (2000) point discussed above.

12. Basic rules regarding the treatment of investments across borders are, of course, features of many trade agreements, including the NAFTA.

13. Of course, it could be that a clearer exposition of the equivalency between these types of labour flows and trade in products between nations could convince the public that it wants neither of them.

14. The CFF was created in 1963 to help nations deal with a sudden and temporary drop in export earnings. It was later modified to assist also in dealing with a sudden rise in import prices of basic cereal foods and for sudden temporary drops in remittances from abroad.

15. The authors are aware of the controversy around the use of Trade Adjustment Assistance (or, for that matter, unemployment compensation); many scholars argue that its availability reduces the incentive for displaced workers to seek new employment, and lengthens unemployment duration. A recent survey of research into Trade Adjustment Assistance – and a description of its history in the United States – can be found in Baiker and Rehavi (2004). Another argument against TAA is that it actually reduces policymakers' incentives to push trade liberalisation. See Magee (2003) as one example.

8. Conclusions: The Future

Peter Coffey and Robert J. Riley

The general overall conclusion to this book is that the reform of the three international institutions, the IMF, the World Bank and the WTO, is both desirable and necessary. Furthermore, this would seem to be a most opportune moment in time to examine this issue and to undertake reform. Having made this observation, it is important to note that whilst there is a general consensus on both sides of the Atlantic that Third World countries should be better represented in the three international organisations and more should be done to help really poverty stricken countries, views do differ on how this should be done. Furthermore, whilst the United States, ever since the publication of the Meltzer Commission Report, has tended to be more active with its proposals for the reform of the IMF and the World Bank, the European Union, has, whilst being concerned with the reform of these two organisations, been particularly concerned with the reform of the workings of the WTO. In fact, it is perhaps notable that in November 2004, the European Parliament issued its third report on the WTO (this report is reproduced as Appendix 3). What, therefore, are the main questions and problems which must be tackled and on which issues is there a meeting of minds between Americans and Europeans?

Regarding both the IMF and the World Bank, there would appear to be a consensus that their roles should be more clearly defined. Here, some would have them revert to their original roles. This, however, would not seem to be exactly feasible since times have changed, and, in the specific case of the World Bank, its role has been largely supplemented or even surpassed by the extraordinary expansion of the international capital markets.

In the specific case of the IMF, whilst there is no consensus on the amount of financial resources to be placed at the Fund's disposal, there seems to be general agreement that good economic and financial governance by debtor nations should be rewarded in some way. Also, there is a general consensus of views that different policies should be applied to different situations in individual countries. Here, the provision of better information – similar to that published by the BIS – is indispensable.

This more individualistic approach also appears to be most desirable in the case of the World Bank. Here, the more frugal conduct and really quite successful example of the European Investment Bank is cited as an organisation (recommended by Europeans) which could serve as a model for the World Bank.

In the case of both the IMF and the World Bank, there are calls both in Europe and South East Asia, for a greater degree of regionalisation. It would seem to be fairly logical for such organisations to have a greater regional personality. Such an evolution should, it is generally agreed, go hand-in-hand with the application of a policy of good governance both at the levels of national economic management and business in general.

Then, there is the need to reform the WTO. Whilst, as has already been noted, the Europeans would appear to be more active than their American cousins in this area, there does nevertheless, appear to be a general consensus of views regarding the need for certain basic reforms. Thus, and particularly in Europe and among Third World countries, there is a desire for greater 'transparency' in the decision-making process. Similarly, there is a general desire for bringing in experts from other disciplines. There is an impression that too much responsibility lies with the trade lawyers who would appear to be oblivious about the 'real' consequences of their decisions. Equally, but particularly on the European side, as, for example, enunciated by Peter Mandelson, the new EU trade commissioner, there is a need for streamlining the decision-making process in the WTO. In fact, in his most recent pronouncement on this matter he spoke of a 'medieval decision-making process'. To date, however, except for calls for a better representation for Third World countries, there have been no clear proposals for reform.

At this point, it is particularly interesting and relevant to note, that at the end of 2004, a study and report was published on the future reform of the United Nations. In this report, a call (which seems to have strong support from both Americans and Europeans, as well as such important countries as Brazil, India and South Africa) is made for an enlargement of and a greater geographical representation in the UN Security Council. This call, at such an important and geographically well-balanced international level would seem to lend support to the authors of this book in their call for the reform of the IMF, the World Bank and the WTO. Whatever the precise outcome of all the different proposals, one thing is almost certain, reform will take place.

Appendix 1. Extract from Peter Coffey (1974), *The World Monetary Crisis*

THE BRETTON WOODS SYSTEM

Two fundamental facts dominate any consideration of the Bretton Woods system. First is the fact of the overpowering strength, in 1944, of the United States economy. This fact was amply demonstrated on the one hand by the adoption by America of the gold exchange standard,[1] and, on the other hand, by the use of the dollar as a currency of intervention. In turn, this economic strength meant that only a plan for international monetary co-operation that received America's support stood any chance of being adopted – hence the adoption of the White Plan rather than the proposals put forward by Keynes.

The important second fact which should not be ignored is that the Bretton Woods system was incomplete. Originally, it was intended to create three world organisations, a clearing union, an investment bank and a world trading organisation. Unfortunately, only the first two organisations were created. From the outset, this insufficiency created a basic gap in the system which has not yet been filled.

THE KEYNES AND WHITE PLANS

The two plans, the Keynes Plan and the White Plan, because of the vision exhibited in the former and the reality shown by the latter, are worthy of our attention.

Regarding one point, both plans were the same – they were concerned exclusively with current account disequilibria. In this respect, they differ fundamentally from SDRs, which may be used both for current and capital account disequilibria. This is really a very important point which appears to have escaped the notice of most economists and which could lead to serious trouble should any nation or nations wish to emulate the practice of the USA in the 1960s in running up major deficits on capital account, thereby exporting inflation to the countries in which American investments were being made.

Keynes was concerned with the dangers inherent in a possible post-war shortage of liquidity. He greatly feared a repetition of the stagnation of the

1930s. Keynes therefore proposed the creation of a large amount of liquidity (about thirty billion dollars), the use of an overdraft principle and the imposition of penalties for surplus countries if they did not use their surpluses. Further novel features of Keynes's plan were the creation of an international unit of currency (the BANCOR), the management of the Fund's activities by representatives of the international intelligentsia and the setting-up of the Fund's headquarters in London and New York.

The White Plan took account of the reality of the fact that the United States would have to finance the Fund heavily and that Congress would therefore demand some say in the choice of criteria adopted. White thus proposed a small amount of liquidity – five billion dollars and the placing of the headquarters of the Fund in Washington. He recommended the use of gold and national currencies and the adoption of a strict deposit principle. The Fund would be managed by representatives of the member states of the organisation.

The basic principles of the White Plan were adopted – though with a somewhat larger liquidity base than was originally proposed. Apart from the use of gold and national currencies in the quota system,[2] the main aims of the system were the maintenance of fixed exchange rates (with a margin of fluctuation of 2 per cent) and the rapid achievement of convertibility. Should a nation judge its balance of payments on current account to be in 'fundamental disequilibrium', it could change the parity of its currency up to 10 per cent without the consent of the Fund. Any change beyond this percentage could only be made with the approval of the Fund.

One of the main aims of the system, the achievement of convertibility, was soon proved to be premature after the disastrous British attempt in 1947. In fact, convertibility for most of the Western currencies was only achieved a good decade later. Also, Keynes's fear regarding the lack of world liquidity was quickly vindicated and only the most substantial and generous provision of Marshall Aid in 1948 prevented the system from collapsing before it even got off the ground. This aid and the period of dollar shortage during the first decade after the Second World War meant that the Fund's activities[3] only really came into being with the Suez Crisis in 1956. Gradually, following this crisis, the shortages of hard currencies other than the dollar become more obvious and were only partly relieved by the General Agreements to Borrow. These arrangements were also symbolic of the gradual change in economic power in the Western world which was to become more acute during the 1960s.

In examining the records of the Bretton Woods system, it is important to stress once more the fact that the system itself is incomplete in that only two of the organisations planned were set up and that these two have at times been somewhat disappointing in their operations.

The quota system has been one of the more questionable elements of the IMF. The national contributions are composed of 25 per cent gold and 75 per cent national currency.[4] These quotas imply at all times that shortages of some currencies and gluts of others are bound to occur. The increases in the quotas made in 1959 were across the board and did not change the basic structure of the quotas. Further, this increase simply took account of price increases in the world.

Until 1969, with the exception of the use of a waiver clause (Article V, Section 4), the members were given access to the Fund's resources – provided that the required currency was available – if:

> The proposed purchase would not cause the Fund's holdings of the purchasing member's currency to increase by more than 25 per cent of its quota during the period of twelve months ending on the date of the purchase nor to exceed 200 per cent of its quota but the 25 per cent limitation shall apply only to the extent that the Fund's holdings of the member's currency have been brought about 75 per cent of its quota if they had been below that amount. (Section 3 (a) (III))

An attempt to give some priority to its members who expected balance-of-payments deficits was the organisation of Standby Arrangements in 1952.

The second of the two bodies, the World Bank or International Bank for Reconstruction and Development (IBRD) has frequently been the subject of criticism because it has been considered that the Bank has conducted its operations at too commercial rates of interest, thus tending to penalise the Third World. It was this criticism which led to the creation by the Bank of the International Development Association (IDA). This organisation makes loans for more social purposes (for example, education) rather than for the basic infrastructure projects as is the case with the World Bank. Further, the loans made by the IDA are normally very long term and carry practically no interest. In this context, after the initial allocations of SDRs had been made in the framework of the IMF, a growing body of opinion considered that in future greater shares of these units should be given to the Third World. Some observers, particularly Lord Kahn, have gone further in suggesting that these increased allocations for the Third World should be channelled through the IDA.

The IMF itself has also been criticised as being a rich man's club. Perhaps as a result of this criticism, the Fund has tended to increase the repayment period for loans made to members from the Third World (the normal period being between three and five years). Also, these countries have been able to increase both the annual and total limits of the shares of their quotas which may be taken out as loans in other currencies.

The end of the decade 1950–60 saw the first signs of decay in the orderly Bretton Woods system.[5] These signs were the source of discussion which increased in vehemence during the 1960s concerning the question whether or not there was too much or too little liquidity in the world. Academics like

Professor Triffin, who questioned the adequacy of world liquidity, nevertheless also questioned (particularly in 1958 and 1959[6]) the strength of the existing system which relied heavily on dollar and sterling liabilities or increases in world liquidity. He considered that the reserves of these countries were inadequate vis-à-vis their liabilities. In the place of the existing system, he proposed the creation of an international unit of account – very similar to Keynes's BANCOR – which would be held in the reserves of central banks and which would be the means of controlling international liquidity.

A more forthright critic of the existing order was M. Rueff of France, who as a disciple of M. Labordère (famous at the beginning of the present century), proposed a return to the gold standard. During the course of the next decade, he coupled this suggestion with his proposal that the official price of gold should be doubled. Subsequent events, both the increase of the price of gold on the free market and the increased purchases of gold by central banks in the late 1960s and early 1970s tended to vindicate the thesis of M. Rueff.

Thus, as the pressures on the pound sterling increased during 1960 and 1961, and as the European Economic Community met with unexpected economic success, it was obvious that the heyday of the Bretton Woods system was a thing of the past and that new arrangements would have to be made for the future. Unfortunately, the decisions taken during the next decade were frequently inadequate in nature and too late in their timing. They thus tended to patch up the existing system and made its collapse not simply inevitable but also more upsetting than it might otherwise have been.

NOTES

1. The United States possessed nearly all the reserves of gold and foreign currency in the West and was thus able to exchange dollars held by central banks at the rate of $35 per ounce.
2. One of the best accounts of the workings of the system is to be found in W.M. Scammell, *International Monetary Policy* (London: Macmillan, 1961).
3. Probably the best account of the record of the Bretton Woods system is to be found in Brian Tew, *International Monetary Co-operation, 1945–70* (London: Hutchinson University Library, 1970).
4. These quotas are in the General Account, the largest being those of Britain and the United States.
5. Most critics would agree that its main success had been the achievement of orderly changes in exchange rates.
6. See R. Triffin, 'The Return to Convertibility: 1926–1931 and 1958–?', *Banca Nazionale del Lavoro, Review*, March 1959.

Source: Peter Coffey (1974), *The World Monetary Crisis*, London: Macmillan.

Appendix 2.   The Meltzer Commission Report, Preface and Executive Summary

PREFACE

In the last two decades, large crises in Latin America, Mexico, Asia, and Russian heightened interest in the structure and functioning of international financial institutions. Calls for additional capital for the International Monetary Fund to respond to these crises raise questions about how the Fund uses resources, whether its advice increases or reduces the severity of crises and its effect on living standards.

Growth in private lending and capital investment, and the expanding objectives of the international development banks, raise questions about the adequacy and effectiveness of these institutions. Repeated commitments to reduce poverty in the poorest nations have not succeeded. A large gap remains between promise and achievement.

Disputes about the functioning of the World Trade Organisation have increased as its role in service industries expanded. Concerns for the environment and the welfare state clash with concerns elsewhere to maintain open trading arrangements, avoid protection, and spur development.

Frequent, large banking crises focus attention on financial fragility, inadequate banking regulation, and the role of the Bank for International Settlements and its affiliated institutions. Are financial standards inadequate? How should they be improved? What should be done to reduce the role of short-term capital in international finance?

In November 1998, as part of the legislation authorising approximately $18 billion of additional funding by the United States for the International Monetary Fund, Congress established the International Financial Institution Advisory Commission to consider the future roles of seven international financial institutions:

the International Monetary Fund,
the World Bank Group,
the Inter-American Development Bank,
the Asian Development Bank,
the African Development Bank,

the World Trade Organisation, and
the Bank for International Settlements.

The Commission was given a six-month life. It held meetings on twelve
days and public hearings on three additional days. All Commission meetings
and hearings were open to the public. And, to make its work accessible to a
broad public, the Commission established an interactive website. All papers
prepared for the Commission and unedited transcripts of all meetings and
public hearings are available on the Commission's website: http://phantom-
x.gsia.cmu.edu/IFIAC. All documents will be published as a permanent record
of the Commission's work.

The Commission did not join the council of despair calling for the
elimination of one or more of these institutions. Nor did it decide to merge
institutions into a larger multi-purpose agency. A large majority agreed that the
institutions should continue if properly reformed to eliminate overlap and
conflict, increase transparency and accountability, return to or assume specific
functions, and become more effective. These changes are most important for
the International Monetary Fund and the multilateral development banks, so
the report directs most attention to those institutions.

Since it had a short life, the Commission relied heavily on people with
expertise gained through years of research or experience working with or for
the seven institutions we were asked to consider. We are grateful to all who
assisted us by writing papers, on very tight deadlines, to inform us and help us
understand the functioning, roles, and responsibilities of these institutions, and
the effects and effectiveness of their programmes. We are grateful, also, for
their suggestions for changes. Many of the authors of commissioned papers
contributed further by testifying before the Commission and by answering
questions. Other witnesses at Commission meetings and public hearings
brought a broad spectrum of opinions that illuminated areas of public concern
or supplemented the information in the commissioned papers. A list of the
witnesses and authors is included at the end of the report.

The members of the Commission benefited also from the opportunity to
meet informally with the Managing Director of the International Monetary
Fund, the Presidents of the World Bank and the Inter-American Development
Bank, the US Executive Directors of the Fund and the Bank, the Secretary of
the Treasury, and their staffs. We are especially grateful to Dr Stanley Fischer,
Acting Managing Director of the International Monetary Fund, and President
James Wolfensohn of the World Bank who presented their views and
responded to questions at one of our hearings.

The Commission operated under Treasury Department rules. We had the
pleasure of working with Mr Timothy Geithner, Ms Caroline Atkinson, Mr
William McFadden, Ms Lauren Vaughan, and many other Treasury personnel.

The Commission's report recommends many far-reaching changes to improve the effectiveness, accountability, and transparency of the financial institutions and to eliminate overlapping responsibilities. These proposals should not be taken as criticism of the individuals who work in and guide these institutions. We have been impressed repeatedly not only by the dedication and commitment of many of the people we met but also by their willingness to assist us, inform us, and supply the information that helped us complete our task.

The Commission depended on the work of a dedicated staff that arranged meetings, organised material, and prepared research reports and drafts of the final report. Their names are listed in the report. Mr Donald R. Sherk, though not a member of the staff, helped us in numerous ways, improved our understanding of the development banks and allowed us to benefit from his long experience and deep knowledge of their problems and prospects.

I am personally grateful to the members of the Commission who worked together in a spirit of comity and harmony, who gave willingly of their time and counsel, and never complained about the heavy demands placed on them. It has been my great pleasure to work with them. Each of them recognised the important contributions that the international financial institutions have made and can make in the future. They joined enthusiastically in this bipartisan study of the stability of the world economy, and the incomes of people in rich and poor countries.

Allan H. Meltzer
Chair
March 2000

VOTES OF THE COMMISSION

The Commission approved the following report by a vote of 8 to 3. Voting affirmative were: Messrs Calomiris, Campbell, Feulner, Hoskins, Huber, Johnson, Meltzer and Sachs. Opposed were: Messrs Bergsten, Levinson and Torres.

The Commission voted unanimously that **(1) the International Monetary Fund, the World Bank and the regional development banks should write-off in their entirety all claims against heavily indebted poor countries (HIPCS) that implement an effective economic and social development strategy in conjunction with the World Bank and the regional development institutions, and (2) the International Monetary Fund should restrict its lending to the provision of short-term liquidity. The current practice of extending long-term loans for poverty reduction and other purposes should end.**

EXECUTIVE SUMMARY: GENERAL PRINCIPLES AND RECOMMENDATIONS FOR REFORM

In November 1998 as part of the legislation authorising $18 billion of additional US funding for the International Monetary Fund, Congress established the International Financial Institution Advisory Commission to recommend future US policy toward seven international institutions: the International Monetary Fund (IMF), the World Bank Group (Bank), the Inter-American Development Bank (IDB), the Asian Development Bank (ADB), the African Development Bank (AfDB), the Bank for International Settlements (BIS), and the World Trade Organisation (WTO).

The economic environment in which the founders expected the IMF and the Bank to function no longer exists. The pegged exchange rate system, which gave purpose to the IMF, ended between 1971 and 1973, after President Nixon halted US gold sales. Instead of providing short-term resources to finance balance of payment deficits under pegged exchange rates, the IMF now functions in a vastly expanded role: as a manager of financial crises in emerging markets, a long-term lender to many developing countries and former Communist countries, an adviser and counsel to many nations, and a collector and disseminator of economic data on its 182 member countries.

Building on their experience in the 1930s, the founders of the Bank believed that the private sector would not furnish an adequate supply of capital to developing countries. The Bank, joined by the regional development banks, intended to make up for the shortfall in resource flows. With the development and expansion of global financial markets, capital provided by the private sector now dwarfs the volume of lending the development banks have done or are likely to do in the future. And, contrary to the initial presumption, most crises in the past quarter century involved not too little but too much lending, particularly short-term lending that proved to be highly volatile.

The frequency and severity of recent crises raise doubts about the system of crisis management now in place and the incentives for private actions that it encourages and sustains. The IMF has given too little attention to improving financial structures in developing countries and too much to expensive rescue operations. Its system of short-term crisis management is too costly, its responses too slow, its advice often incorrect, and its efforts to influence policy and practice too intrusive.

High cost and low effectiveness characterise many development bank operations as well. The World Bank's evaluation of its own performance in Africa found a 73 per cent failure rate.[1] Only one of four programmes, on average, achieved satisfactory, sustainable results. In reducing poverty and promoting the creation and development of markets and institutional structures that facilitate development, the record of the World Bank and the regional development banks leaves much room for improvement.

The Commission's Aims

In 1945, the United States espoused an unprecedented definition of a nation's interest. It defined its position in terms of the peace and prosperity of the rest of the world. It differentiated the concepts of interest and control. This was the spirit which created the International Financial Institutions and which has guided the Commission's work. Global economic growth, political stability and the alleviation of poverty in the developing world are in the national interest of the United States.

The Commission believes that performance of the IMF, the Bank, and the regional banks would improve considerably if each institution was more accountable and had a clearer focus on an important, but limited, set of objectives. Further, the IMF, the Bank, and the regional banks should change their operations to reduce the opportunity for corruption in recipient countries to a minimum.

Accountability, accomplishment, effectiveness, and reduction in corruption will not be achieved by hope, exhortation, and rhetoric. Programmes must be restructured to change incentives for both recipients and donor institutions. Each institution should have separate functions that do not duplicate the responsibilities and activities of other institutions. The IMF should continue as crisis manager under new rules that give member countries incentives to increase the safety and soundness of their financial systems. For the Bank and the regional banks, emphasis should be on poverty reduction and development not, as in the past, on the volume of lending.

IMF

The IMF should serve as quasi lender of last resort to emerging economies. However, its lending operations should be limited to the provision of liquidity (that is, short-term funds) to solvent member governments when financial markets close. Liquidity loans would have short maturity, be made at a penalty rate (above the borrower's recent market rate) and be secured by a clear priority claim on the borrower's assets. Borrowers would not willingly pay the penalty rate if financial markets would lend on the same security, so resort to the IMF would be reduced. It would serve as a stand-by lender to prevent panics or crises. Except in unusual circumstances, where the crisis poses a threat to the global economy, loans would be made only to countries in crisis that have met pre-conditions that establish financial soundness. To the extent that IMF lending is limited to short-term liquidity loans, backed by pre-conditions that support financial soundness, there would be no need for detailed conditionality (often including dozens of conditions) that has burdened IMF programmes in recent years and made such programmes unwieldy, highly conflictive, time consuming to negotiate, and often ineffectual.

Four of the proposed pre-conditions for liquidity assistance that we recommend are: First, to limit corruption and reduce risk by increasing portfolio diversification, **eligible member countries must permit, in a phased manner over a period of years, freedom of entry and operation for foreign financial institutions**. Extensive recent history has demonstrated that emerging market economies would gain from increased stability, a safer financial structure, and improved management and market skills brought by the greater presence of foreign financial institutions in their countries. A competitive banking system would limit use of local banks to finance 'pet projects', or lend to favoured groups on favourable terms, thereby reducing the frequency of future financial crises.

Second, to encourage prudent behaviour, safety and soundness **every country that borrows from the IMF must publish, regularly and in a timely manner, the maturity structure of its outstanding sovereign and guaranteed debt and off-balance sheet liabilities**. Lenders need accurate information on the size of the short-term liabilities to assess properly the risks that they undertake.

Third, **commercial banks must be adequately capitalised either by a significant equity position, in accord with international standards, or by subordinated debt held by non-governmental and unaffiliated entities**. Further, the IMF in cooperation with the BIS should promulgate new standards to ensure adequate management of liquidity by commercial banks and other financial institutions so as to reduce the frequency of crises due to the sudden withdrawal of short-term credit.

Fourth, **the IMF should establish a proper fiscal requirement to assure that IMF resources would not be used to sustain irresponsible budget policies**.

To give countries time to adjust to these incentives for financial reform, **the new rules should be phased in over a period of five years. If a crisis occurred in the interim, countries should be allowed to borrow from the IMF at an interest rate above the penalty rate**.

Maintenance of stabilising budget and credit policies is far more important that the choice of exchange rate regime. **The Commission recommends that countries avoid pegged or adjustable rate systems**. The IMF should use its policy consultations to recommend either firmly fixed rates (currency board, dollarisation) or fluctuating rates. Neither fixed nor fluctuating rates are appropriate for all countries or all times. Experience shows, however, that mixed systems such as pegged rates or fixed but adjustable rates increase the risk and severity of crises.

Long-term structural assistance to support institutional reform and sound economic policies would be the responsibility of the Bank and the regional banks. **The IMF should cease lending to countries for long-term development assistance (as in sub-Saharan Africa) and for long-term structural transformation (as in the post-Communist transition economies).** The Enhanced Structural Adjustment Facility and its successor, the Poverty Reduction and Growth Facility, should be eliminated.

The IMF should write-off in entirety its claims against all heavily indebted countries (HIPCS) that implement an effective economic development strategy in conjunction with the World Bank and the regional development institutions.

In keeping with the greatly reduced lending role of the IMF, the Commission recommends against further quota increases for the foreseeable future. The IMF's current resources should be sufficient for it to manage its quasi lender of last resort responsibilities, especially as current outstanding credits are repaid to the IMF.

The Development Banks

At the entrance to the World Bank's headquarters in Washington, a large sign reads: 'Our dream is a world without poverty.' The Commission shares that objective as a long-term goal. Unfortunately, neither the World Bank nor the regional development banks are pursuing the set of activities that could best help the world move rapidly toward that objective or even the lesser, but more fully achievable, goal of raising living standards and the quality of life, particularly for people in the poorest nations of the world.

Collectively, the World Bank Group and its three regional counterparts employ 17,000 people in 170 offices around the world, have obtained $500 billion in capital from national treasuries, hold a loan portfolio of $300 billion and each year extend a total of $50 billion in loans to developing members.

There is a wide gap between the banks' rhetoric and promises and their performance and achievements. The World Bank is illustrative. In keeping with a mission to alleviate poverty in the developing world, the Bank claims to focus its lending on the countries most in need of official assistance because of poverty and lack of access to private sector resources. Not so. Seventy per cent of the World Bank non-aid resources flow to 11 countries that enjoy substantial access to private resource flows.

The regional institutions overlap with the World Bank in several ways. They compete for donor funds, clients and projects. Their local offices are often in the same cities. The regionals repeat the World Bank's organisational structure, which focuses on subsidised loans and guarantees to governments, zero-interest credits to the poorest members, and loans, guarantees and equity capital for private sector operations. Recently, the World Bank expanded its field offices, increasing duplication and potential conflict in the regions. The Commission received no reasonable explanation of why this costly expansion was chosen instead of closer cooperation with the regional banks and reliance on the regional banks' personnel.

All the banks operate at the country level, defining their objectives within the nation-states instead of the region or the globe. Their patterns of lending over the past 3 years are very similar to the same countries and for the same purposes. Four to six of the most credit-worthy borrowers all with easy capital market access, receive most non-aid resource flows: 90 per cent in Asia; 80–90 per cent in Africa; 75–85 per cent in Latin America.

Performance is one of the Commission's principal concerns. Ending or reducing poverty is not easy. The development banks cannot succeed in their mission unless the countries choose institutions and government policies that support growth. Developing country governments must be willing to make institutional changes that promote improved social conditions, reward domestic innovation and saving, and attract foreign capital. To foster an environment conducive to economic growth, the development banks must change their internal incentives and the incentives they offer developing countries.

The project evaluation process at the World Bank gets low marks for credibility: wrong criteria combined with poor timing. Projects are rated on three measures: outcome, institutional development impact and sustainability. The latter, central to progress in the emerging world, receives a minimal average 5 per cent weight in the overall evaluation. Results are measured at the moment of final disbursement of funds. Evaluation should be a repetitive process spread over many years, including well after the final disbursement of funds when an operational history is available.

The banks seldom return to inspect project success or assess sustainability of results. After auditing 25 per cent of its projects, the World Bank reviews only 5 per cent of its programmes 3 to 10 years after final disbursement for broad policy impact. Though the development banks devote significant resources to monitoring procurement of inputs, they do little to measure the effectiveness of outputs over time.

Recommendations for the Development Banks

To function more effectively, the development banks must be transformed from capital-intensive lenders to sources of technical assistance, providers of regional and global public goods, and facilitators of an increased flow of private sector resources to the emerging countries. Their common goal should be to reduce poverty: their individual responsibilities should be distinct. Their common effort should be to encourage countries to attract productive investment; their individual responsibility should be to remain accountable for their performance. Their common aim should be to increase incentives that assure effectiveness. The focus of their individual financial efforts should be on the 80 to 90 poorest countries of the world that lack capital market access.

All resource transfers to countries that enjoy capital market access (as denoted by an investment grade international bond rating) or with a per capita income in excess of $4000, would be phased out over the next 5 years. Starting at $2500 (per capita income), official assistance would be limited. (Dollar values should be indexed.) Emergency lending would be the responsibility of the IMF in its capacity as quasi lender of last resort. This recommendation assures that development aid adds to available resources (additionality).

Performance-Based Grants

For the world's truly poor, the provision of improved levels of health care, primary education and physical infrastructure, once the original focus for development funding, should again become the starting points for raising living standards. Yet, poverty is often most entrenched and widespread in countries where corrupt and inefficient governments undermine the ability to benefit from aid or repay debt. Loans to these governments are, too often, wasted, squandered, or stolen.

In poor countries without capital market access, poverty alleviation grants to subsidise user fees should be paid directly to the supplier upon independently verified delivery of service. Grants should replace the traditional Bank tools of loans and guarantees for physical infrastructure and social service projects. Grant funding should be increased if grants are used effectively.

From vaccinations to roads, from literacy to water supply, services would be performed by outside private sector providers (including NGOs and charitable organisations) as well as by public agencies. Service contracts would be awarded on competitive bid. Quantity and quality of performance would be verified by independent auditors. Payments would be made directly to suppliers. Costs would be divided between recipient countries and the development agency. The subsidy would vary between 10 per cent and 90 per cent, depending upon capital market access and per capita income.

Institutional Reform Loans

Institutional reforms lay the groundwork for productive investment and economic growth. They provide the true long-term path to end poverty. Reforms are more likely to succeed if they arise from decisions made by the developing country.

Lending frameworks, with incentives for implementation, should be redesigned to fit the needs of the poorest countries that do not have capital market access. The government of each developing economy would present its own reform programme. If the development agency concurs in the merit of the proposal, the country would receive a loan with a subsidised interest rate. The extent of the interest rate subsidy would range from 10 per cent to 90 per cent, as in grant financing of user fees. **Lending for institutional reform in poor countries without capital market access should be conditional upon implementation of specific institutional and policy changes and supported by financial incentives to promote continuing implementation.** Auditors, independent of both the borrowing government and the official lender, would be appointed to review implementation of the reform programme annually.

Division of Responsibility

To underscore the shift in emphasis from lending to development, the name of the World Bank would be changed to World Development Agency. Similar changes should be made at the regional development banks.

Development Agencies should be precluded from financial crisis lending.

All country and regional programmes in Latin America and Asia should be the primary responsibility of the area's regional bank.

The World Bank should become the principal source of aid for the African continent until the African Development Bank is ready to take full responsibility. The World Bank would also be the development agency responsible for the few remaining poor countries in Europe and the Middle East.

Regional solutions that recognise the mutual concerns of interdependent nations should be emphasised.

The World Development Agency should concentrate on the production of global public goods and serve as a centre for technical assistance to the regional development agencies. Global public goods include treatment of tropical diseases and AIDS, rational protection of environmental resources, tropical climate agricultural programmes, development of

management and regulatory practices, and inter-country infrastructure.

In its reduced role, the World Development Agency would have less need for its current callable capital. Some of the callable capital should be reallocated to regional development agencies, and some should be reduced in line with a declining loan portfolio. The income from paid-in capital and retained earnings should be reallocated to finance the increased provision of global public goods. Independent evaluations of the agencies' effectiveness should be published annually.

Debt Reduction and Grant Aid to the Poorest Countries

The World Bank and the regional development banks should write off in entirety their claims against all heavily indebted poor countries (HIPCS) that implement an effective economic development strategy under the Banks' combined supervision. Moreover, bilateral creditors, such as the US government, should similarly extend full debt write-offs to those HIPC countries that pursue effective economic development strategies.

More generally, the **United States should be prepared to increase significantly its budgetary support for the poorest countries if they pursue effective programmes of economic development**. This support should come in several forms: debt reduction, grants channelled through the multilateral development agencies, and bilateral grant aid. The current level of US budgetary support for the poorest countries is about $6 per US citizen ($1.5 billion total), so there is scope for a significant increase in funding if justified by appropriate policies and results within the developing countries.

The Bank for International Settlements

During its 70-year history the BIS has adapted well to large changes in the financial industry and central banking practices. Its ability to adapt was due largely to its limited and homogeneous membership. An example of such adaptation is the way the BIS quickly rose to the challenge of meeting regulatory deficiencies at the international level. The BIS has also demonstrated its ability to convince the most financially important countries to adopt its standards.

The Commission recommends that the BIS remain a financial standard setter. Implementation of standards, and decisions to adopt them, should be left to domestic regulators or legislatures. The Basel Committee on Bank Supervision should align its risk measures more closely with credit and market risk. Current practice encourages misallocation of lending.

The World Trade Organisation

The WTO has two main functions. First, it administers the process by which trade rules change. Trade ministers (or their equivalent) negotiate agreements that national legislative bodies can approve or reject. Second, the WTO serves as a quasi-judicial body to settle disputes. Part of this process involves the use of sanctions against countries that violate trade rules.

Quasi-judicial determination, when coupled with the imposition of sanctions, can overwhelm a country's legislative process. As WTO decisions move to the broader range of issues now within its mandate, there is considerable risk that WTO rulings will override national legislation in areas of health, safety, environment, and other regulatory policies. The Commission believes that quasi-judicial decisions of international organisations should not supplant national legislative enactments. The system of checks and balances between legislative, executive and judicial branches must be maintained.

Rulings or decisions by the WTO, or any other multilateral entity, that extend the scope of explicit commitments under treaties or international agreements must remain subject to explicit legislative enactment by the US Congress and, elsewhere, by the national legislative authority.

NOTE

1.   Based on World Bank data from the Bank's web site.

Source: International Financial Institution Advisory Commission (2000), *The Meltzer Commission Final Report: The Future of the IMF and the World Bank*, Washington, DC: International Financial Institution Advisory Commission.

Appendix 3

BULLETIN QUOTIDIEN EUROPE
(5 AUGUST 2004)

Doha Development Programme: Results of Negotiations at WTO General Council

During the night of 31 July to 1 August after arduous negotiation, the 147 member nations of the World Trade Organisation (WTO) adopted, in Geneva, a framework agreement to reactivate the Doha Development Programme after talks failed in Cancún in autumn 2003. The decision taken by the WTO General Council is published in our EUROPE/Documents series, in French and English. (On the subject of negotiations in Geneva, see EUROPE of 3 August, p. 4, and also 29 July, p. 5; 30 July, p. 7; and 31 July, p. 6.)

****

DRAFT GENERAL COUNCIL DECISION OF 31 JULY 2004

1. The General Council reaffirms the Ministerial Declarations and Decisions adopted at Doha and the full commitment of all Members to give effect to them. The Council emphasizes Members' resolve to Doha. Taking into account the Ministerial Statement adopted at Cancún on 14 September 2003, and the statements by the Council Chairman and the Director-General at the Council meeting of 15–16 December 2003, the Council takes note of the report by the Chairman of the Trade Negotiations Committee (TNC) and agrees to take action as follows:

   (a) **Agriculture:** the General Council adopts the framework set out in Annex A to this document.

   (b) **Cotton:** the General Council reaffirms the importance of the Sectoral Initiative on Cotton and takes note of the parameters set out in Annex A within which the trade-related aspects of this issue will be pursued in the agricultural negotiations. The General Council also attaches importance to the development aspects of the Cotton Initiative and wishes to stress the complementarity between the trade and development aspects. The Council takes note of the recent Workshop on Cotton in Cotonou on 23–24 March 2004 organized by the WTO Secretariat, and other bilateral and multilateral efforts to make progress on the development assistance aspects and instructs the Secretariat to continue to work with the development community and to provide the Council with periodic reports on relevant developments.

Members should work on related issues of development multilaterally with the international financial institutions, continue their bilateral programmes, and all developed countries are urged to participate. In this regard, the General Council instructs the Director-General to consult with the relevant international organizations, including the Bretton Woods Institutions, the Food and Agricultural Organization and the International Trade Centre to direct effectively existing programmes and any additional resources towards development of the economies where cotton has vital importance.

(c) **Non-agricultural Market Access:** the General Council adopts the framework set out in Annex B to this document.

(d) **Development:**

Principles: development concerns form an integral part of the Doha Ministerial Declaration. The General Council rededicates and recommits Members to fulfilling the development dimension of the Doha Development Agenda, which places the needs and interests of developing and least-developed countries at the heart of the Doha Work Programme. The Council reiterates the important role that enhanced market access, balanced rules, and well targeted, sustainably financial technical assistance and capacity building programmes can play in the economic development of these countries.

Special and Differential Treatment: the General Council reaffirms that provisions for special and differential (S&D) treatment are an integral part of the WTO Agreements. The Council recalls Ministers' decision in Doha to review all S&D treatment provisions with a view to strengthening them and making them more precise, effective and operational. The Council recognizes the progress that has been made so far. The Council instructs the Committee on Trade and Development in Special Session to expeditiously complete the review of all the outstanding Agreement-specific proposals and report to the General Council, with clear recommendations for a decision, by July 2005. The Council further instructs the Committee, within the parameters of the Doha mandate, to address all other outstanding work, including on the cross-cutting issues, the monitoring mechanism and the incorporation of S&D treatment into the architecture of WTO rules, as referred to in TN/CTD/7 and report, as appropriate, to the General Council.

The Council also instructs all WTO bodies to which proposals in Category II have been referred to expeditiously complete the consideration of these proposals and report to the General Council, with clear recommendations for a decision, as soon as possible and no later than July 2005. In doing so these bodies will ensure that, as far as possible, their meetings do not overlap so as to enable full and effective participation of developing countries in these discussions.

Technical Assistance: the General Council recognizes the progress that has been made since the Doha Ministerial Conference in expanding Trade-Related Technical Assistance (TRTA) to developing countries and low-income countries in transition. In furthering this effort the Council affirms that such countries, and in particular least-developed countries, should be provided with enhanced TRTA and capacity building, to increase their effective participation in the negotiations, to facilitate their implementation of WTO rules, and to enable them to adjust and diversify their economies. In this context the Council welcomes and further encourages the improved coordination with other agencies, including under the Integrated Framework for TRTA for the LDCs (IF) and the Joint Integrated Technical Assistance Programme (JITAP).

Implementation: concerning implementation-related issues, the General Council reaffirms the mandates Ministers gave in paragraph 12 of the Doha Ministerial Declaration and the Doha Decision on Implementation-Related Issues and Concerns, and renews Members' determination to find appropriate solutions as a priority. Without prejudice to the position of Members, the Council requests the Director-General to continue with his consultative process on all outstanding implementation issues under paragraph 12(b) of the Doha Ministerial Declaration, including on issues related to the extension of the protection of geographical indications provided for in Article 23 of the TRIPS agreement to products other than wines and spirits, if need be by appointing Chairpersons of concerned WTO bodies as his Friends and/or by holding dedicated consultations. The Director-General shall report to the TNC and the General Council no later than May 2005. The Council shall review progress and take any appropriate action no later than July 2005.

Other Development Issues: in the ongoing market access negotiations, recognising the fundamental principles of the WTO and relevant provisions of GATT 1994, special attention shall be given to the specific trade- and development-related needs and concerns of developing countries, including relating to food security, rural development, livelihood, preferences, commodities and net food imports, as well as prior unilateral liberalisation, should be taken into consideration, as appropriate, in the course of the Agriculture and MAMA negotiations. The trade-related issues identified for the fuller integration of small, vulnerable economies into the multilateral trading system, should also be addressed, without creating a sub-category of Members, as part of a work programme, as mandated in paragraph 35 of the Doha Ministerial Declaration.

Least Developed Issues: the General Council reaffirms the commitments made at Doha concerning least-developed countries and renews its determination to fulfil these commitments. Members will continue to take due account of the concerns of least-developed countries in the negotiations. The Council confirms that nothing in this Decision shall detract in any way from the special provisions agreed by Members in respect of these countries.

(e) **Services:** the General Council takes note of the report of the TNC by the Special Session of the Council for Trade in Services (2) and reaffirms Members' commitment to progress in this area of the negotiations in line with the Doha mandate. The Council adopts the recommendations agreed by the Special Session, set out in Annex C to this document, on the basis of which further progress in the services negotiations will be pursued. Revised offers should be tabled by May 2005.

(f) **Other Negotiating Bodies:**

Rules, Trade & Environment and TRIPS: the General Council takes note of the reports to the TNC by the Negotiating Group on

Rules and by the Special Sessions of the Committee on Trade and Environment and the TRIPS Council (3). The Council reaffirms Members' commitment to progress in all of these areas of the negotiations in line with the Doha mandates.

Dispute Settlement: the General Council takes note of the report to the TNC by the Special Session of the Dispute Settlement Body (4) and reaffirms Members' commitment to progress in this area of the negotiations in line with the Doha mandate. The Council adopts the TNC's recommendation that work in the Special Session should continue on the basis set out by the Chairman of that body in his report to the TNC.

(g) **Trade Facilitation:** taking note of the work done on trade facilitation by the Council for Trade in Goods under the mandate in paragraph 27 of the Doha Ministerial Declaration and for the work carried out under the auspices of the General Council both prior to the Fifth Ministerial Conference and after its conclusion, the General Council decides by explicit consensus to commence negotiations on the basis of the modalities set out in Annex D to this document.

Relationship between Trade and Investment, Interaction between Trade and Competition Policy and Transparency in Government Procurement: the Council agrees that these issues, mentioned in the Doha Ministerial Declaration in paragraphs 20–22, 23–25 and 26 respectively, will not form part of the Work Programme set out in the Declaration and therefore no work towards negotiations on any of these issues will take place within the WTO during the Doha Round.

(h) **Other Elements of the Work Programme:** the General Council reaffirms the high priority Ministers at Doha gave to those elements of the Work Programme which do not involve negotiations. Noting that a number of these issues are of particular interest to developing country Members, the Council emphasises its commitment to fulfil the mandates given by Ministers in all these areas. To this end, the General Council and other relevant bodies shall report in line with their Doha mandates to the Sixth Session of the Ministerial Conference. The moratoria covered by paragraph 11.1 of the Doha Ministerial Decision on Implementation-related Issues and Concerns and paragraph 34 of the Doha Ministerial Declaration are extended up to the Sixth Ministerial Conference.

2.   The General Council agrees that this Decision and its Annexes shall not be used in any dispute settlement proceeding under the DSU and shall not be used for interpreting the existing WTO Agreements.

3.   The General Council calls on all Members to redouble their efforts towards the conclusion of a balanced overall outcome of the Doha Development Agenda in fulfilment of the commitments Ministers took at Doha. The Council agrees to continue the negotiations launched at Doha beyond the timeframe set out in paragraph 45 of the Doha Declaration, leading to the Sixth Session of the Ministerial Conference. Recalling its decision of 21 October 2003 to accept the generous offer of the Government of Hong Kong, China to host the Sixth Session, the Council further agrees that this Session will be held in December 2005.

****

Annex A

Framework for Establishing Modalities in Agriculture

1.   The starting point for the current phase of the agriculture negotiations has been the mandate set out in Paragraph 13 of the Doha Ministerial Declaration. This in turn built on the long-term objective of the Agreement on Agriculture to establish a fair and market-orientated trading system through a programme of fundamental reform. The elements below offer the additional precision required at this stage of the negotiations and thus the basis for the negotiations of full modalities in the next phase. The level of ambition set by the Doha mandate will continue to be the basis for the negotiations on agriculture.

2.   The final balance will be found only at the conclusion of these subsequent negotiations and within the Single Undertaking. To achieve this balance, the modalities to be developed will need to incorporate operationally effective and meaningful provisions for special and differential treatment for developing country Members. Agriculture is of critical importance to the economic development of developing country Members and they must be able to pursue agricultural policies that are supportive of their development goals, poverty reduction strategies, food security and livelihood concerns. Non-trade concerns, as referred to in Paragraph 13 of the Doha Declaration, will be taken into account.

3.   The reforms in all three pillars form an interconnected whole and must be approached in a balanced and equitable manner.

4. The General Council recognizes the importance of cotton for a certain number of countries and its vital importance for developing countries, especially LDCs. It will be addressed ambitiously, expeditiously, and specifically, within the agriculture negotiations. The provisions of this framework provide a basis for this approach, as does the sectoral initiative on cotton. The Special Session of the Committee on Agriculture shall ensure appropriate prioritisation of the cotton issue independently from other sectoral initiatives. A subcommittee on cotton will meet periodically and report to the Special Session of the Committee on Agriculture to review progress. Work shall encompass all trade-distorting policies affecting the sector in all three pillars of market access, domestic support, and export competition, as specified in the Doha text and Framework text.

5. Coherence between trade and development aspects of the cotton issue will be pursued as set out in paragraph 1.b of the text to which this Framework is annexed.

DOMESTIC SUPPORT

6. The Doha Ministerial Declaration calls for 'substantial reductions in trade-distorting domestic support'. With a view to achieving these substantial reductions, the negotiations in this pillar will ensure the following:

    •   Special and differential treatment remains an integral component of domestic support. Modalities to be developed will include longer implementation periods and lower reduction coefficients for all types of trade-distorting domestic support and continued access to the provisions under Article 6.2.

    •   There will be a strong element of harmonisation in the reductions made by developed Members. Specifically, higher levels of permitted trade-distorting domestic support will be subject to deeper cuts.

    •   Each such Member will make a substantial reduction in the overall level of its trade-distorting support from bound levels.

    •   As well as this overall commitment, Final Bound Total AMS and permitted de minimis levels will be subject to substantial reductions and, in the case of the Blue Box, will be capped as specified in paragraph 15 in order to ensure results that are coherent with the long-term reform objective. Any clarification or development rules and conditions to govern trade distorting support will take this into account.

Overall Reduction: A Tiered Formula

7. The overall base level of all trade-distorting domestic support, as measured by the Final Bound Total AMS plus permitted de minimis level agreed in paragraph 8 below for Blue Box payments, will be reduced according to a tiered formula. Under this formula, Members having higher levels of trade-distorting domestic support will make greater overall reductions in order to achieve a harmonising result. As the first instalment of the overall cut, in the first year and throughout the implementation period, the sum of all trade-distorting support will not exceed 80 per cent of the sum of Final Bound Total AMS plus permitted de minimis plus the Blue Box at the level determined in paragraph 15.

8. The following parameters will guide the further negotiation of this tiered formula:

    •   This commitment will apply as a minimum overall commitment. It will not be applied as a ceiling on reductions of overall trade-distorting domestic support, should the separate and complementary formulae to be developed for Total AMS, de minimis and Blue Box payments imply, when taken together, a deeper cut in overall trade-distorting domestic support for an individual Member.

    •   The base for measuring the Blue Box component will be the higher of existing Blue Box payments during a recent representative period to be agreed and the cap established in paragraph 15 below.

Final Bound Total AMS: A Tiered Formula

9. To achieve reductions with harmonising effect:

    •   Final Bound Total AMS will be reduced substantially, using a tiered approach.

    •   Members having higher Total AMS will make greater reductions.

    •   To prevent circumvention of the objective of the Agreement through transfers of unchanged domestic support between different support categories, product-specific AMSs will be capped at their respective average levels according to a methodology to be agreed.

- Substantial reductions in Final Bound Total AMS will result in reductions of some product-specific support.

10. Members may make greater than formula reductions in order to achieve the required level of cut in overall trade-distorting domestic support.

De Minimis

11. Reductions in de minimis will be negotiated taking into account the principle of special and differential treatment. Developing countries that allocate almost all de minimis support for subsistence and resource-poor farmers will be exempt.

12. Members may make greater than formula reductions in order to achieve the required level of cut in overall trade-distorting domestic support.

Blue Box

13. Members recognise the role of the Blue Box in promoting agricultural reforms. In this light, Article 6.5 will be reviewed so that Members may have recourse to the following measures:

- Direct payments under production-limiting programmes if:

  o such payments are based on fixed and unchanging areas and yields; or

  o such payments are made on 85 per cent or less of a fixed and unchanging base level of production; or

  o livestock payments are made on a fixed and unchanging number of head. Or

- Direct payments that do not require production if:

  o such payments are based on fixed and unchanging bases and yields; or

  o livestock payments made on a fixed and unchanging number of head; and

  o such payments are made on 85 per cent or less of a fixed and unchanging base level of production

14. The above criteria, along with additional criteria will be negotiated. Any such criteria will ensure that Blue Box payments are less trade-distorting than AMS measures, it being understood that:

    • Any new criteria would need to take account of the balance of WTO rights and obligations.

    • Any new criteria to be agreed will not have the perverse effect of undoing ongoing reforms.

15. Blue Box support will not exceed 5 per cent of a Member's average total value of agricultural production during an historical period. The historical period will be established in the negotiations. This ceiling will apply to any actual or potential Blue Box user from the beginning of the implementation period. In cases where a Member has placed an exceptionally large percentage of its trade-distorting support in the Blue Box, some flexibility will be provided on a basis to be agreed to ensure that such a Member is not called upon to make a wholly disproportionate cut.

Green Box

16. Green Box criteria will be reviewed and clarified with a view to ensuring that Green Box measures have no, or at most minimal, trade-distorting effects or effects on production. Such a review and clarification will need to ensure that the basic concepts, principles and effectiveness of the Green Box remain and take due account of non-trade concerns. The improved obligations for monitoring and surveillance of all new disciplines foreshadowed in paragraph 48 below will be particularly important with respect to the Green Box.

EXPORT COMPETITION

17. The Doha Ministerial Declaration calls for 'reduction of, with a view to phasing out, all forms of export subsidies'. As an outcome for the negotiations, Members agree to establish detailed modalities ensuring the parallel elimination of all forms of export subsidies and disciplines on all export measures with equivalent effect by a credible end date.

End Point

18. The following will be eliminated by the end date to be agreed:

    • Export subsidies are scheduled.

- Export credits, export credit guarantees or insurance programmes with repayment periods beyond 180 days.

- Terms and conditions relating to export credits, export credit guarantees or insurance programmes with repayment periods of 180 days and below which are not in accordance with disciplines to be agreed. These disciplines will cover, inter alia, payment of interest minimum interest rates, minimum premium requirements, and other elements which can constitute subsidies or otherwise distort trade.

- Trade-distorting practices with respect to exporting STEs including eliminating export subsidies provided to or by them, government financing, and the underwriting losses. The issue of the future use of monopoly powers will be subject to further negotiation.

- Provision of food aid that is not in conformity with operationally effective disciplines to be agreed. The objective of such disciplines will be to prevent commercial displacement. The role of international organizations as regards to the provision of food aid by Members, including related humanitarian and developmental issues, will be addressed in the negotiations. The question of providing food aid exclusively in fully grant form will also be addressed in negotiations.

19. Effective transparency provisions for paragraph 18 will be established. Such provisions, in accordance with standard WTO practice, will be consistent with commercial confidentiality considerations.

Implementation

20. Commitments and disciplines in paragraph 18 will be implemented according to a schedule and modalities to be agreed. Commitments will be implemented by annual instalments. Their phasing will take into account the need for some coherence with internal reform steps of members.

21. The negotiation of the elements in paragraph 18 and their implementation will ensure equivalent and parallel commitments by Members.

Special and Differential Treatment

22. Developing country Members will benefit from longer implementation periods for the phasing out of all forms of export subsidies.

23. Developing countries will continue to benefit from special and differential treatment under the provisions of Article 9.4 of the Agreement on Agriculture for a reasonable period, to be negotiated, after the phasing out of all forms of export subsidies and implementation of all disciplines identified above are completed.

24. Members will ensure that the disciplines on export credits, export credit guarantees or insurance programmes to be agreed will make appropriate provision for differential treatment in favour of least-developed and net food-importing developing countries as provided for in paragraph 4 of the Decision on Measures Concerning the Possible Negative Effects of the Reform Programme on Least-Developed and Net Food-Importing Developing Countries. Improved obligations for monitoring and surveillance of all new disciplines as foreshadowed in paragraph 48 will be critically important in this regard. Provisions to be agreed in this respect must not undermine the commitments undertaken by Members under the obligations in paragraph 18 above.

25. STEs in developing country Members which enjoy special privileges to preserve domestic consumer price stability and to ensure food security will receive special consideration for maintaining monopoly status.

Special Circumstances

26. In exceptional circumstances, which cannot be adequately covered by food aid, commercial export credits or preferential international financing facilities, ad hoc temporary financing arrangements relating to exports to developing countries may be agreed by Members. Such agreements must not have the effect of undermining commitments undertaken by Members in paragraph 18 above, and will be based on criteria and consultation procedures to be established.

MARKET ACCESS

27. The Doha Ministerial Declaration calls for 'substantial improvements in market access'. Members also agreed that special and differential treatment for developing country Members would be an integral part of all elements in the negotiations.

The Single Approach: A Tiered Formula

28. To ensure that a single approach for developed and developing country Members meets all the objectives of the Doha mandate, tariff reductions

will be made through a tiered formula that takes into account their different tariff structures.

29. To ensure that such a formula will lead to substantial trade expansion, the following principles will guide its further negotiation:

   - Tariff reductions will be made from bound rates. Substantial overall tariff reductions will be achieved as a final result from negotiations.

   - Each Member (other than LDSs) will make a contribution. Operationally effective special and differential provisions for developing country Members will be an integral part of all elements.

   - Progress in tariff reductions will be achieved through deeper cuts in higher tariffs with flexibilities for sensitive products. Substantial improvements in market access will be achieved for all products.

30. The number of bands, the thresholds for defining the bands and the type of tariff reduction in each band remain under negotiation. The role of a tariff cap in a tiered formula with distinct treatment for sensitive products will be further evaluated.

Sensitive Products

Selection

31. Without undermining the overall objective of the tiered approach, Members may designate an appropriate number, to be negotiated, of tariff lines to be treated as sensitive, taking account of existing commitments for these products.

Treatment

32. The principle of 'substantial improvement' will apply to each product.

33. 'Substantial improvement' will be achieved through combinations of tariff quota commitments and tariff reductions applying to each product. However, balance in this negotiation will be found only if the final negotiated result also reflects the sensitivity of the product concerned.

34. Some MFN-based tariff quota expansion will be required for all such products. A base for such an expansion will be established, taking account of coherent and equitable criteria to be developed in the negotiations. In order not to undermine the objective of the tiered approach, for all such products, MFN-based tariff quota expansion will be provided under specific rules to be negotiated taking into account deviations from the tariff formula.

Other Elements

35. Other elements that will give the flexibility required to reach a final balanced result include reduction or elimination of in-quota tariff rates, and operationally effective improvements in tariff quota administration for existing tariff quotas so as to enable Members, and particularly developing country Members, to fully benefit from the market access opportunities under tariff rate quotas.

36. Tariff escalation will be addressed through a formula to be agreed.

37. The issue of tariff simplification remains under negotiation.

38. The question of special agricultural safeguard (SSG) remains under negotiation.

Special and Differential Treatment

39. Having regard to their rural development, food security and/or livelihood security needs, special and differential treatment for developing countries will be an integral part of all elements of the negotiation, including the tariff reduction formula, the number and treatment of sensitive products, expansion of tariff rate quotas, and implementation period.

40. Proportionality will be achieved by requiring lesser tariff reduction commitments or tariff quota expansion commitments from developing country Members.

41. Developing country Members will have the flexibility to designate an appropriate number of products as Special Products, based on criteria of food security, livelihood security and rural development needs. These products will be eligible for more flexible treatment. The criteria and treatment of these products will be further specified during the

negotiation phase and will recognize the fundamental importance of Special Products to developing countries.

42. A Special Safeguard Mechanism (SSM) will be established for use by developing country Members.

43. Full implementation of long-standing commitment to achieve the fullest liberalisation of trade in tropical agricultural products of particular importance to the diversification of production from the growing of illicit narcotic crops is overdue and will be addressed effectively in the market access negotiations.

44. The importance of long-standing preferences is fully recognised. The issue of preference erosion will be addressed. For the further consideration in this regard, paragraph 16 and other relevant provisions of TN/AG/W/1Rev.1 will be used as a reference.

LEAST-DEVELOPED COUNTRIES

45. Least-developed Countries, which will have full access to all special and differential treatment provisions above, are not required to undertake reduction commitments. Development Members, and developing country Members in a position to do so, should provide duty-free and quota-free market access for products originating from least-developed countries.

46. Work on cotton under all the pillars will reflect the vital importance of this sector to certain LDC Members and we will work to achieve ambitious results expeditiously.

RECENTLY ACCEDED MEMBERS

47. The particular concerns of recently acceded Members will be effectively addressed through specific flexibility provisions.

MONITORING AND SURVEILLANCE

48. Article 18 of the Agreement on Agriculture will be amended with a view to enhancing monitoring so as to effectively ensure full transparency, including through timely and complete notifications with respect to the commitments in market access, domestic support and export competition. The particular concerns of developing countries in this regard will be addressed.

OTHER ISSUES

49.   Issues of interest but not agreed: sectoral initiatives, differential export taxes, GIs.

50.   Disciplines on export prohibitions and restrictions in Article 12.1 of the Agreement on Agriculture will be strengthened.

****

Annex B

Framework for Establishing Modalities in Market Access For Non-Agricultural Products

1.   This Framework contains the initial elements for future work on modalities by the Negotiating Group on Market Access. Additional negotiations are required to reach agreement on the specifics of some of these elements. These relate to the formula, the issues concerning the treatment of unbound tariffs in indent two of paragraph 5, the flexibilities for developing-country participants, the issue of participation in the sectorial tariff component and the preferences. In order to finalise the modalities, the Negotiating Group is instructed to address these issues expeditiously in a manner consistent with the mandate of paragraph 16 of the Doha Ministerial Declaration and the overall balance therein.

2.   We reaffirm that negotiations on market access for non-agricultural products shall aim to reduce or as appropriate eliminate tariffs, including the reduction or elimination of tariff peaks, high tariffs, and tariff escalation, as well as non-tariff barriers, in particular on products of export interest to developing countries. We also reaffirm the importance of special and differential treatment and less than full reciprocity in reduction commitments as integral parts of the modalities.

3.   We acknowledge the substantial work undertaken by the Negotiating Group on Market Access and the progress towards achieving an agreement on negotiating modalities. We take note of the constructive dialogue on the Chair's Draft Elements of Modalities (TN/MA/W/35/Rev.1) and confirm our intention to use this document as a reference for the future work of the Negotiating Group. We instruct the Negotiating Group to continue its work, as mandated by paragraph 16 of the Doha Ministerial Declaration with its corresponding references to the relevant provisions of

Article XXVIII bis of GATT 1994 and to the provisions cited in paragraph 50 of the Doha Ministerial Declaration, on the basis set out below.

4. We recognize that a formula approach is key to reducing tariffs, and reducing or eliminating tariff peaks, high tariffs, and tariff escalation. We agree that the Negotiating Group should continue its work on a non-linear formula applied on a line-by-line basis which shall take fully into account the special needs and interests of developing and least-developed country participants, including through less than full reciprocity in reduction commitments.

5. We further agree on the following elements regarding the formula:

    ● product coverage shall be comprehensive without a priori exclusions;

    ● tariff reductions or elimination shall commence from the bound rates after full implementation of current concessions; however, for unbound tariff lines, the basis of commencing the tariff reductions shall be [two] times the MFN applied rate in the base year;

    ● the base year for MFN applied tariff rates shall be 2001 (applicable rates on 14 November);

    ● credit shall be given for autonomous liberalization by developing countries provided that the tariff lines were bound on an MFN basis in the WTO since the conclusion of the Uruguay Round;

    ● all non-ad valorem duties shall be converted to ad valorem equivalents on the basis of a methodology to be determined and bound in ad valorem terms;

    ● negotiations shall commence on the basis of the HS96 or HS2002 nomenclature, with the results of the negotiations to be finalised in HS2002 nomenclature;

    ● the reference period for import data shall be 1999–2001.

6. We furthermore agree that, as an exception, participants with a binding coverage of non-agricultural tariff lines of less than [35] per cent would be exempt from making tariff reductions through the formula. Instead, we expect them to bind [100] per cent of non-agricultural tariff lines at an average level that does not exceed the overall average of bound tariffs for all developing countries after full implementation of current concessions.

7. We recognise that a sectoral tariff component, aiming at elimination or harmonisation is another key element to achieving the objectives of paragraph 16 of the Doha Ministerial Declaration with regard to the reduction or elimination of tariffs, in particular on products of export interest to developing countries. We recognise that participation by all participants will be important to that effect. We therefore instruct the Negotiating Group to pursue its discussions on such a component, with a view to defining product coverage, participation, and adequate provisions of flexibility for developing-country participants.

8. We agree that developing-country participants shall have longer implementation periods for tariff reductions. In addition, they shall be given the following flexibility:

   (a) applying less than formula cuts to up to [10] per cent of the tariff lines provided that the cuts are no less than half the formula cuts and that these tariff lines do not exceed [10] per cent of the total value of a Member's imports; or

   (b) keeping, as an exception, tariff lines unbound, or not applying formula cuts for up to [5] per cent of tariff lines provided they do not exceed [5] per cent of the total value of a Member's imports.

   We furthermore agree that this flexibility could not be used to exclude entire HS Chapters.

9. We agree that least-developed country participants shall not be required to apply the formula nor participate in the sectoral approach, however, as part of their contribution to this round of negotiations, they are expected to substantially increase their level of binding commitments.

10. Furthermore, in recognition of the need to enhance the integration of least-developed counties into the multilateral trading system and support the diversification of their production and export base, we call upon developed-country participants and other participants who so decide, to grant on an autonomous basis duty-free and quota-free market access for non-agricultural products originating from least-developed countries by the year [...].

11. We recognise that newly acceded Members shall have recourse to special provisions for tariff reductions in order to take into account their extensive market access commitments undertaken as part of their

accession and that stage tariff reductions are still being implemented in many cases. We instruct the Negotiating Group to further elaborate on such provisions.

12.   We agree that newly acceded Members shall have recourse to special provisions for tariff reductions in order to take into account their extensive market access commitments undertaken as part of their accession and that stage tariff reductions are still being implemented in many cases. We instruct the Negotiating Group to further elaborate on such provisions.

13.   In addition, we ask developed-country participants and other participants who so decide to consider the elimination of low duties.

14.   We recognise that NTBs are an integral and equally important part of these negotiations and instruct participants to intensify their work on NTBs. In particular, we encourage all participants to make notifications on NTBs by 31 October 2004 and to proceed with identification, examination, categorisation, and ultimately negotiations on NTBs. We take note that the modalities for addressing NTBs in these negotiations could include request/offer, horizontal, or vertical approaches; and should fully take into account the principle of special and differential treatment for developing and least-developed country participants.

15.   We recognise that appropriate studies and capacity building measures shall be an integral part of the modalities to be agreed. We also recognise the work that has already been undertaken in these areas and ask participants to continue to identify such issues to improve participation in the negotiations.

16.   We recognise the challenges that may be faced by non-reciprocal preference beneficiary Members and those Members that are at present highly dependent on tariff revenue as a result of these negotiations on non-agricultural products. We instruct the Negotiating Group to take into consideration, in the course of its work, the particular needs that may arise for the Members concerned.

17.   We furthermore encourage the Negotiating Group to work closely with the Committee on Trade and Environment in Special Session with a view to addressing the issue of non-agricultural environmental goods covered in paragraph 31 (iii) of the Doha Ministerial Declaration.

****

Annex C

Recommendations of the Special Session of the Council for Trade in Services

(a) Members who have not yet submitted their initial offers must do so as soon as possible.

(b) A date for the submission of a round of revised offers should be established as soon as feasible.

(c) With a view to providing effective market access to all Members and in order to ensure a substantive outcome, Members shall strive to ensure a high quality of offers, particularly in sectors and modes of supply of export interest to developing countries, with special attention to be given to least-developed countries.

(d) Members shall aim to achieve progressively higher levels of liberalisation with no a priori exclusion of any service sector or mode of supply and shall give special attention to sectors and modes of supply of export interest to developing countries. Members note the interest of developing countries, as well as other Members, in Mode 4.

(e) Members must intensify their efforts to conclude the negotiations on rule-making under GATS Articles VI:4, X, XIII and XV in accordance with their respective mandates and deadlines.

(f) Targeted technical assistance should be provided with a view to enabling developing countries to participate effectively in the negotiations.

(g) For the purpose of the Sixth Ministerial meeting, the Special Session of the Council for Trade in Services shall review progress in these negotiations and provide a full report to the Trade Negotiations Committee, including possible recommendations.

****

Annex D

Modalities for Negotiations on Trade Facilitation

1. Negotiations shall aim to clarify and improve relevant aspects of Articles V, VIII and X of the GATT 1994 with a view to further expediting the

movement, release and clearance of goods, including goods in transit (5). Negotiations shall also aim at enhancing technical assistance and support for capacity building in this area. The negotiations shall further aim at provisions for effective cooperation between customs or any other appropriate authorities on trade facilitation and customs compliance issues.

2. The results of the negotiations shall take fully into account the principle of special and differential treatment for developing and least-developed countries. Members recognise that this principle should extend beyond the granting of traditional transition periods for implementing commitments. In particular, the extent and the timing of entering into commitments shall be related to the implementation capacities of developing and least-developed members. It is further agreed that those Members would not be obliged to undertake investments in infrastructure projects beyond their means.

3. Least-developed country Members will only be required to undertake commitments to the extent consistent with their individual development, financial and trade needs or their administrative and institutional capabilities.

4. As an integral part of the negotiations, Members shall seek to identify their trade facilitation needs and priorities, particularly those of developing and least-developed countries, and shall also address the concerns of developing countries related to cost implications of proposed measures.

5. It is recognised that the provision of technical assistance and support for capacity building is vital for developing and least-developed countries to enable them to fully participate in and benefit from the negotiations. Members, in particular developed countries, therefore commit themselves to adequately ensure such support and assistance during the negotiations (6).

6. Support and assistance should also be provided to help developing and least-developed countries implement the commitments resulting from the negotiations, in accordance with their nature and scope. In this context, it is recognised that negotiations could lead to certain commitments whose implementation would require support for infrastructure development on the part of some Members. In these limited cases, developed-country Members will make every effort to ensure support and assistance directly

related to the nature and scope of the commitments in order to allow implementation. It is understood, however, that in cases where required support and assistance for such infrastructure is not forthcoming, and where a developed-country Member continues to lack the necessary capacity, implementation will not be required. While every effort will be made to ensure the necessary support and assistance, it is understood that the commitments by developed countries to provide such support are not open-ended.

7. Members agree to review the effectiveness of the support and assistance provided and its ability to support the implementation of the results of the negotiations.

8. In order to make technical assistance and capacity building more effective and operational and to ensure better coherence, Members shall invite relevant international organizations, including the IMF, OECD, UNCTAD, WCO and the World Bank to undertake a collaborative effort in this regard.

9. Due account shall be taken of the relevant work of the WCO and other relevant international organizations in this area.

10. Paragraphs 45–51 of the Doha Ministerial Declaration shall apply to these negotiations. At its first meeting after the July session of the General Council, the Trade Negotiations Committee shall establish a Negotiating Group on Trade Facilitation and appoint its Chair. The first meeting of the Negotiating Group shall agree on a work plan and schedule of meetings.

BULLETIN QUOTIDIEN EUROPE
(1 DECEMBER 2004)

Third Parliamentary Conference on the WTO
(24–26 November in Brussels)

The third session of the Parliamentary Conference on the WTO, organised by the European Parliament and the Interparliamentary Union, was held from 24 to 26 November in Brussels (see EUROPE of 27 November, p. 11 and 30 November, p. 9). Parliamentarians of the World Trade Organisation's member countries adopted on this occasion a declaration that is published in full in our series EUROPE/Documents (in French and English).

Final Declaration

1. We parliamentarians assembled in Brussels for the annual session of the Parliamentary Conference on the WTO, welcome the July 2004 declaration of the WTO General Council concerning the Doha Work Programme. The July package has raised hopes that the impasse of the Ministerial Conference in Cancún has finally been overcome, with a consensual roadmap now in place for moving the multilateral trade negotiations forward.

2. While we are encouraged by the renewed momentum, numerous grey areas must still be clarified in the negotiations in order to ensure a positive end result. Significant differences mark the positions of WTO Members on issues currently in dispute. Determination and political will to fulfil commitments are therefore required of all parties in order to bring the Doha Round to a successful conclusion. Parliaments bear a central share of responsibility in this respect.

3. We reiterate our commitment to the promotion of free and fair trade that benefits people everywhere, enhances sustainable development and reduces poverty. As legitimate representatives of our populations, we shall continue to oversee WTO activities and promote their effectiveness and fairness, keeping in mind the original objectives of the WTO, as set out in the Marrakesh Agreement.

4. To be successful, WTO negotiations must involve all members of the Organization at all stages, and their overall results should permit consistency between national policy objectives and faithful adherence to international obligations. To that end, there should be a genuine balance

of benefit for all WTO Members and acceding countries, ensuring fair and equitable relationships between exporting countries, importing countries as well as between developed countries and developing, with special emphasis placed on ensuring real gains for developing countries, and especially the least-developed countries.

5. We stress the importance of lower industrial tariffs in particular to provide improved market access for developing countries, especially LDCs, better market access for non-agricultural goods, and trade facilitation. Clear progress in these areas is needed to help the world trade system to function better and more effectively.

6. We welcome the July decision on agriculture and call on WTO Members to continue working on the three pillars of the negotiation, namely:

   - elimination of all forms of export subsidies;
   - substantial reduction in trade-distorting domestic support; and
   - market access.

7. We are keenly aware of the existence of complex areas in **agriculture negotiations** that are of direct concern to producers and consumers, exporters and importers alike. They reflect the critical importance of agriculture to the economic development and growth prospects of the majority of WTO Members and a real step in the right direction, which has to be further elaborated. The Framework for Establishing Modalities in Agriculture, adopted by the WTO General Council on 31 July 2004, fills in some details in this regard, but leaves most of the hard decisions to future negotiations, with no specified deadlines. It is fundamental to define and provide a framework for the notion of 'sensitive product' and for the issues of special interest to developing countries such as special safeguard mechanism and special products for developing countries, as stated in the 31 July Agreement. There is also a need to discuss further sectoral initiatives, differential export taxes and geographical indications.

8. Clear progress in these areas is needed to help the world trade system to function better and more effectively. We note in this regard that the so-called 'peace clause' has expired, and that WTO Members are now free to exercise their right to challenge breaches of the rules. We believe that recourse to such challenges should be used sparingly, with the aim of encouraging the withdrawal of export subsidies while avoiding the introduction of further tension and distractions at this stage of the negotiations.

9.   We urge the WTO and its members to make information available as
      extensively as possible on national commitments in the agricultural
      sector that extend over the timeframe of these negotiations and have a
      direct bearing on the three reform pillars, as set out in the Framework,
      namely market access, domestic support, export competition. This
      information would provide a transparent backdrop for all Members, but
      especially developing countries.

10.   We attach the highest importance to the pressing needs of developing
      countries dependent on tropical agricultural commodity exports, notably
      sugar, bananas and cotton. Each of these has been the subject of
      disputes in the WTO. Consideration should be also given to the
      situation of developing countries dependent on export incomes from
      coffee, cocoa, pineapple, rice, and other monocultures. Strict attention
      should be paid to the specific trade, finance and development needs of
      developing countries, as enshrined first in the GATT and now in the
      WTO.

11.   At each step of the ongoing negotiations, including those on regional
      trade arrangements, the concerns of developing countries in respect of
      poverty reduction, food security and sustainable livelihoods must be kept
      at the forefront. In order to enable the coexistence of the diverse
      agricultural systems of various countries, non-trade concerns of
      agriculture which include food security, land conservation, revitalisation
      of rural society and rural employment, as well as the issues of
      sustainable forestry and fisheries must also be addressed in a satisfactory
      manner.

12.   Hunger and famine are still ravaging the poorest people in many
      countries. The issues of malnutrition and hunger deserve sharper focus
      in the negotiations on export competition. We emphasise in this regard
      on the one hand the responsibility of developed countries, which produce
      and export the bulk of food commodities and secondly the need, and
      indeed the obligation, for developing countries to promote bold,
      proactive rural development policies in earnest. The solution to food
      security problems may lie in a complementary relationship to be sought
      between developed countries, which should endeavour to support local
      production and regional markets in developing countries, and the
      developing countries themselves, which should set up the necessary
      production and marketing arrangements for agricultural commodities
      with a view to gradually meeting their food needs. The special
      negotiations for which disciplines and commitments are to be negotiated

must be clear, flexible and provide food-importing countries with the necessary leeway to protect and promote national food security. There is also a need to take a close look at the Food Aid Convention, the FAO consultative surplus disposal mechanism and the FAO/WHO *Codex Alimentarius.*

13. We welcome the fact that the Framework gives special attention to the least-developed countries. We support the proposal that the developed countries, and those developing countries that are in a position to do so, should provide duty-free and quota-free market access for products originating from the least-developed countries.

14. We note with satisfaction that cotton was given prominence in the Framework, and that a subcommittee has been established by the WTO and given the mandate to 'achieve ambitious results expeditiously'. We call on all parties concerned to ensure that these results reach the farmers in the developing countries in a timely manner.

15. Given the growing importance of the services sector in all economies and the expansion of **trade in services**, including the movement of natural persons and the cross-border provision of services, we acknowledge the decision of the WTO General Council to approve a number of recommendations aimed at advancing the negotiations on trade in services, the overall pace of which remains disappointing. Revised offers must be submitted by WTO Members in this regard by mid-2005, with the aim of satisfying the concerns of all countries concerned.

16. At the same time, caution must be exercised in the liberalisation of trade in services, especially those that relate to basic human rights and basic essential services and needs such as public health, education, culture, and social services: liberalisation of such services should not be imposed by wealthier countries, nor should it be used in negotiations on export subsidies. This approach is consistent with key principles of the GATS, which allow for flexibility in opening services sectors to competition and for the exclusion of some sectors in whole or in part. Longer time frames for the implementation of market access will provide the necessary measure of margin for those developing countries where the institutional arrangements are weak and the negotiations on completing the rules are still unfinished. We also believe that every country has the right to protect its cultural diversity and to conserve and develop public services.

17. We stress the need to continue making progress in the area of TRIPS and taking action against counterfeiting and piracy by promoting fair forms of competition. We underline the importance of technical assistance to developing countries to implement the TRIPS rules. Special attention should be given to the protection of biodiversity and access to essential low cost medicines.

18. We are convinced that **trade-related capacity-building** through appropriately delivered technical assistance should remain an indispensable element of the current negotiations. Increased awareness leads on the one hand to more active participation by all WTO Members in the negotiations, and on the other hand to better understanding of the relevant issues across the widest national spectrum, including members of parliament. This makes the outcome of trade negotiations more likely to be acceptable.

19. We note in this regard that the commitments made at the Doha Ministerial Conference in 2001 are being followed up through increased activities by the donor countries, the WTO and other multilateral bodies. We encourage all parties to do more to build the essential human, institutional and economic capacities required to prepare for, negotiate and sustain the implementation of the WTO rules and disciplines. Special attention should be devoted in this regard to the needs of parliaments, particularly in developing countries, which should become active partners in trade agreements.

20. We are convinced that parliaments can make substantial contributions to the WTO negotiations. Parliaments embody the sovereignty and can legitimately contribute to expressing the will of the people in international fora and promoting popular support for international agreements. We call on parliaments and their members to help raise citizens' awareness and understanding of trade negotiations and the WTO. We urge governments and parliaments to engage in a regular dialogue so that the latter can effectively exercise parliamentary oversight of the international trade negotiations and their follow-up.

21. We decide to hold the next session of the Parliamentary Conference at the WTO on the occasion of the Sixth WTO Ministerial Conference, in Hong Kong (13–18 December 2005). We call upon all WTO Members to include members of parliament in their official delegations at the Ministerial Conference. We also call on our respective governments participating in that Conference to add the following paragraph to the

final declaration: 'Transparency of the WTO should be enhanced by associating parliaments closely with the activities of the WTO.'

22. We instruct the IPU and the European Parliament to take the steps required, in the Steering Committee, to ensure that this declaration is followed up in the WTO Secretariat.

Source: EUROPE/Documents Nos 2376–7, 1 December 2004, Brussels: Agence Europe.

Bibliography

AFL–CIO (American Federation of Labor–Congress of Industrial Organisations) (2005), 'What is the WTO?', Policy Statement.

Anand, P.B. (2004), 'Financing the provision of global public goods', *The World Economy*, February, **27** (2), 215–37.

Ardito-Barletta, Nicolas (1994), 'Managing development and transition', in Peter B. Kenan (ed.), *Managing the World Economy: Fifty Years after Bretton Woods*, Washington, DC: Institute for International Economics, pp. 173–200.

Askari, Hossein (2004), 'Global financial governance: whose ownership?', *Business Economics*, April, **34**, 57–62.

Bagwell, Kyle and Robert Staiger (1999), 'Domestic policies, national sovereignty and international economics institutions', National Bureau of Economic Research Working Paper 7293, August.

Bagwell, Kyle, Petros C. Mavroidis and Robert W. Staiger (2002), 'It's a question of market access', *American Journal of International Law*, January, **96** (1), 56–76.

Baiker, Katherine and M. Marit Rehavi (2004), 'Policy watch: trade adjustment assistance', *Journal of Economic Perspectives*, Spring, **18** (2), 239–55.

Barro, Robert J. (2000), 'If we can't abolish the IMF, let's at least make big changes', *Business Week*, 10 April, p. 28.

Berger, A.N., W.C. Hunter and S.G. Timme (1993), 'The efficiency of financial institutions: a review of research past, present, and future', *Journal of Banking and Finance*, April, **17**, 221–49.

Bhagwhati, Jagdish (2002), 'Afterword: the question of linkage', *American Journal of International Law*, January, **96** (1), 126–34.

Bhagwhati, Jagdish (2004), *In Defense of Globalization*, New York: Oxford University Press.

Bird, Graham (2001), 'IMF programs: do they work? Can they be made to work better?', *World Development*, November, **29** (11), 1849–65.

Boot, Arnoud W.A., Todd T. Milbourn and Anjan V. Thakor (2002), 'Evolution of organizational scale and scope: does it ever pay to get bigger and less focused?,' April 16, working paper, Washington University, St. Louis.

Bretton Woods Commission (1994), *Bretton Woods: Looking to the Future*, July, Commission Report.

Bretton Woods Committee (2003), 'The World Trade Organization: should we retool or restructure?', *Critical Issues Forum*.

Calomiris, Charles W. (1999), 'How to invent a new IMF', *The International Economy*, January/February, 32–5.

Calomiris, Charles W. (2000), 'When will economics guide IMF and World Bank reforms?', *Cato Journal*, **20** (1), Spring/Summer, 85–103.

Calomiris, Charles W. and Allan H. Meltzer (1999), 'Fixing the IMF', *The National Interest*, Summer, 88–94.

Carbo, S., E.P.M. Gardener and J. Williams (2002), 'Efficiency in banking: empirical evidence from the savings banks sector', *The Manchester School*, March, **70** (2), 204–26.

Charnovitz, Steve (2002), 'Triangulating the World Trade Organization', *American Journal of International Law*, January, **96** (1), 28–55.

Clark, Jeffrey A. and Paul J. Speaker (1994), 'Economies of scale and scope in banking: evidence from a generalized translog cost function', *Quarterly Journal of Business and Economics*, Spring, **33** (2), 3–25.

Diamond, Jared (1999), *Guns, Germs, and Steel: The Fates of Human Societies*, New York/London: W.W. Norton & Company.

Ederington, Josh (2001), 'International coordination of trade and domestic policies', *American Economic Review*, December, 1580–93.

Ederington, Josh (2002), 'Trade and domestic policy linkage in international agreements', *International Economic Review*, **43** (4), 1347–67.

Edwards, Sebastian (1998), 'Abolish the IMF', *The Financial Times*, November 13.

Eichengreen, Barry (1999), 'Strengthening the international financial architecture: where do we stand?', October, University of California-Berkeley working paper.

Eichengreen, Barry (2004), 'Financial instability', Copenhagen Consensus Challenge Paper, April.

Einhorn, Jessica (2001), 'The World Bank's mission creep', *Foreign Affairs*, **80** (5), Sept/Oct, 22–7.

Feinberg, Richard E. (1988), 'The changing relationship between the World Bank and the International Monetary Fund', *International Organization*, Summer, **42** (3), 545–60.

Feldstein, Martin S. (1998), 'Refocusing the IMF', *Foreign Affairs*, March–April, **77** (2), 20–25.

Goldstein, Morris (2001), 'An evaluation of proposals to reform the international financial architecture', March, NBER conference paper.

Graham, Carol and Paul Masson (2000), 'The IMF's dilemma in Argentina: time for a new approach to lending?', The Brookings Institution Policy Brief, no. 111, November.

Group of Seven Finance Ministers (2001), 'Strengthening the international financial architecture', report from G7 Finance Ministers to the Heads of State and Government, 8 July.

Huang, Tai-Hsin and Mei-Hui Wang (2004), 'Estimation of scale and scope economies in multiproduct banking: evidence from the Fourier flexible functional form with panel data', *Applied Economics*, 20 June, **36** (11), 1245–53.

International Financial Institution Advisory Commission (2000), *The Meltzer Commission Final Report: The Future of the IMF and the World Bank*, Washington, DC: International Financial Institution Advisory Commission.

International Monetary Fund (2002a), 'The design of the sovereign debt restructuring mechanism – further considerations', Washington, DC, November.

International Monetary Fund (Independent Evaluation Office) (2002b), 'Evaluation of the prolonged use of fund resources', Washington, DC, September.

International Monetary Fund (2003a), *Report of the Managing Director to the International Monetary and Financial Committee on the IMF's Policy Agenda*, Washington, DC, 11 April.

International Monetary Fund (Independent Evaluation Office) (2003b), 'Evaluation report: fiscal adjustment in IMF-supported programs', Washington, DC, September.

International Monetary Fund and World Bank (2004), 'Financing modalities toward the Millennium Development Goals: a progress note', Joint Ministerial Commission, 25 April.

Irwin, Douglas A. (2000), 'Do we need the WTO?', *Cato Journal*, Winter, **19** (3), 351–7.

Jackson, John (1994), 'Managing the trading system: the World Trade Organization and the post-Uruguay Round GATT agenda', in Peter B. Kenan (ed.), *Managing the World Economy: Fifty Years after Bretton Woods*, Washington, DC: Institute for International Economics, pp. 131–71.

Jackson, John H. (2002), 'Afterword: the linkage problem – comments on five texts', *American Journal of International Law*, January, **96** (1), 118–25.

Kaul, Inge and Katell Le Goulven (2003), 'Financing global public goods: a new frontier of public finance', in Kaul et al. (eds), *Providing Global Public Goods: Managing Globalization*, New York: Oxford University Press, pp. 329–71.

Kaul, Inge, Pedro Conceição, Katell Le Goulven and Ronald U. Mendoza (eds) (2003), *Providing Global Public Goods: Managing Globalization*, New York: Oxford University Press.

Kenen, Peter B. (ed.) (1994), *Managing the World Economy: Fifty Years after Bretton Woods*, Washington, DC: Institute for International Economics.

Kenen, Peter B. (2002), 'The international financial architecture: old issues and new initiatives', *International Finance*, April, **5** (1), 23–45.

Kindleberger, Charles P. *(2000), Manias, Panics, and Crashes: A History of Financial Crises*, 4th edn, New York: John Wiley & Sons, Inc.

Krueger, Anne O. (1998), 'Whither the World Bank and the IMF?', *Journal of Economic Literature*, **36** (4), December, 1983–2020.

Krueger, Anne O. (2002a), 'New approaches to sovereign debt restructuring: an update on our thinking', Conference on Sovereign Debt Workouts: Hopes and Hazards, Washington, DC: Institute for International Economics, April.

Krueger, Anne O. (2002b), 'Sovereign debt restructuring and dispute resolution', Washington, DC, Bretton Woods Committee Annual Meeting, 6 June.

Krugman, Paul (2003), 'Crying with Argentina', in *The Great Unraveling: Losing Our Way in the New Century*, New York and London: Houghton Mifflin & Company, pp. 353–5.

Landes, David S. (1998), *The Wealth and Poverty of Nations: Why Some Are so Rich and Some Are so Poor*, New York and London: W.W. Norton & Company.

Lash, William H. (2000), 'WTO Report Card II: an exercise or surrender of U.S. sovereignty?', Trade Briefing Paper 4, Cato Institute: Center for Trade Policy Studies.

Leebron, David W. (2002), 'Linkages', *American Journal of International Law*, January, **96** (1), 5–27.

Magee, Christopher (2001), 'Administered protection for workers: an analysis of the Trade Adjustment Assistance Program', *Journal of International Economics*, February, **53** (1), 105–25.

Magee, Christopher (2003), 'Endogenous tariffs and trade adjustment assistance', *Journal of International Economics*, **60** (1), May, 203–22.

McQuillan, Lawrence J. (1998), 'Essays in Public Policy: The Case Against the International Monetary Fund', The Hoover Institution, Stanford University.

Meltzer, Allan H. (1999), 'What's wrong with the IMF? What could be better?', in William C. Hunter, George G. Kaufman and Thomas Krueger (eds), *The Asian Financial Crisis: Origins, Implications, and Solutions*, Boston: Kluwer Academic Publishing, pp. 241–60.

Mikesell, Raymond F. (2000), 'Bretton Woods – original intentions and current problems', *Contemporary Economic Policy*, **18** (4), October, 404–14.

Mokhiber, Russell and Robert Weissman (1999), 'Ten reasons to dismantle the WTO', http://www.jacksonprogressive.com/issues/mokhiberweissman/tenreasons112399.html, November.

Odell, John S. (2001), 'Problems in negotiating consensus in the World Trade

Organization', paper presented at the American Political Science Association Meetings, 30 August.

Radelet, Steven and Jeffrey Sachs (1998), *The Onset of the East Asian Financial Crisis*, Harvard Institute for International Development.

Ranis, Gustav (1994), 'Defining the mission of the World Bank Group', in *Bretton Woods: Looking to the Future*, Bretton Woods Commission Report, July.

Richardson, J. David (2001), 'Designing a market enhancing WTO', in Alan M. Rugman and Gavin Boyd (eds), *The World Trade Organization in the New Global Economy*, Cheltenham, UK and Northampton, MA, USA: Edward Elgar, pp. 257–74.

Rodrik, Dani (2001), 'Four simple principles for democratic governance of globalization', Harvard University working paper, May.

Rodrik, Dani (2002), 'Feasible globalizations', Harvard University working paper, July.

Rodrik, Dani (2003), 'Growth strategies', CEPR discussion paper 4100, October.

Rodrik, Dani, Arvind Subramanian and Francesco Trebbi (2002), 'Institutions rule: the primacy of institutions over geography and integration in economic development', CEPR discussion paper 3643, October.

Rogoff, Ken (2003a), 'The IMF strikes back', *Foreign Policy*, January/February, **134**, 39–47.

Rogoff, Kenneth (2003b), 'More cheerleading or more whistle-blowing? A little more whistle-blowing would be a welcome sound', *Finance & Development*, Washington, DC: The IMF, September, 56–7.

Rogoff, Kenneth (2004), 'The sisters at 60', *The Economist*, 22 July, 63–6.

Rose, Andrew K. (2003), 'Which international institutions promote international trade?', CEPR discussion paper 3764, January.

Rueff, Jacques (1975), *La Réforme du Système Monétaire International*, October, Paris: Plon.

Rugman, Alan M. (2001), 'The World Trade Organization and the international political economy', in Alan M. Rugman and Gavin Boyd, *The World Trade Organization in the New Global Economy*, Cheltenham, UK and Northampton, MA, USA: Edward Elgar, pp. 1–21.

Rugman, Alan M. and Gavin Boyd (2001), *The World Trade Organization in the New Global Economy*, Cheltenham, UK and Northampton, MA, USA: Edward Elgar.

Ruttan, Vernon W. (1998), 'The new growth theory and development economics: a survey', *Journal of Development Studies*, December, **35** (2), 1–18.

Ryrie, William (1994), 'Reshaping the development task in a world of market economies', in *Bretton Woods: Looking to the Future*, Bretton Woods

Commission Report, July.

Sandler, Todd (1998), 'Global and regional public goods: a prognosis for collective action', *Fiscal Studies*, August, **19** (3), 221–47.

Sandler, Todd (2001), 'On financing global and international public goods', University of Southern California working paper, July.

Schott, Jeffrey J. (ed.) (2000), *The WTO after Seattle*, Washington, DC: Institute for International Economics.

Schott, Jeffrey (2003), 'The World Trade Organization: should we restructure or retool?', *The Bretton Woods Committee Critical Issues Forum*, p. 8.

Schwartz, Anna J. (2000), 'Do we need a new Bretton Woods?', *Cato Journal*, Spring/Summer, **20** (1), 21–5.

Soros, George (1998), *The Crisis of Global Capitalism: Open Society Endangered*, New York: PublicAffairs.

Soros, George (2002), *On Globalization*, New York: PublicAffairs.

Srinivasan, T.N. (2003), 'The World Trade Organization: should we restructure or retool?', *The Bretton Woods Committee Critical Issues Forum*, p. 9.

Steger, Debra P. (2002), 'Afterword: the 'trade and ...' conundrum – a commentary', *American Journal of International Law*, January, **96** (1), 135–45.

Stern, Paula (2003), 'The World Trade Organization: should we restructure or retool?', *The Bretton Woods Committee Critical Issues Forum*, pp. 10–11.

Stiglitz, Joseph (2002), *Globalization and Its Discontents*, New York and London: W.W. Norton & Company.

Subramanian, Arvind and Shang-Jin Wei (2003), 'The WTO promotes trade, strongly but unevenly', National Bureau of Economic Research working paper 10024, October.

Summers, Lawrence (1994), 'Shared prosperity and the new international economic order', in Peter B. Kenan (ed.), *Managing the World Economy: Fifty Years after Bretton Woods*, Washington, DC: Institute for International Economics, pp. 419–26.

USTR (United States Trade Representative) (2001), *Background Information on the WTO*.

US Treasury (2000), *Response to the Report of the International Financial Institution Advisory Commission*, Washington, DC: U.S. Treasury, 8 June.

World Bank (2003), 'Global economic prospects: realizing the development potential of the Doha Round', Washington, DC: IRBD/World Bank.

World Bank (2004), 'Policies and actions for achieving the Millenium Development Goals and related outcomes', The Global Monitoring Report, Washington, DC: The International Reconstruction and Development Bank/World Bank.

World Trade Organisation (2003), 'Coherence in global economic policymaking and cooperation between the WTO, the IMF, and the World Bank', Note by the Secretariat, Document WT/TF/COH/S/7, 20 April.

World Trade Organization (2004), 'Coherence in the global economic policy-making: WTO cooperation with the IMF and World Bank', October.

Zoellick, Robert B. (2001), 'The WTO and new global trade negotiations: what's at stake?', Speech to the Council of Foreign Relations, Washington, DC, 31 October.

Index